Beginning Programming with Liberty BASIC
First Edition

By Carl Gundel
Copyright 2009 Shoptalk Systems

ISBN 978-0-557-22811-9

To my wife Flor, and to my daughters Laurie and Melody.
– for your love and support

Table of Contents

Chapter One

A Hairy Short History of Programming - An Urban Legend

Programming languages have been around for almost as long as we have had general purpose computers (meaning computers that can be reconfigured to do different things). People have always needed some way to express their ideas into a plan for the computer to execute. This is really important because computers are not very smart. You can't just speak to them and tell them what to do like we see people do in movies. This makes them hard to program. People were pulling their hair out! One shiny-headed computer user's wife was overheard saying, "Something must be done!" The rest is history.

Even before modern hair replacement techniques, programming languages were the answer to a balding computer staff. Countless programming languages have been designed. Some languages are designed to solve a special kind of problem, some are created just to suit the whims of their designers, and some are designed to be especially good at regrowing hair. [Editors note - "Hey, it works for me!"]

Here is a short list of languages just to give a taste. This list doesn't scratch the surface.

Language	Introduced	Commonly used for
Assembly	Mid 1950's	General purpose
LISP	1956	Artificial Intelligence
FORTRAN	1957	Scientific computing
COBOL	1959	Business programming
BASIC	1964	General purpose
Forth	1970	Machine control
Pascal	1970	Education
Smalltalk	1971	General purpose
C	1972	System level programming
Java	1995	General purpose
Perl	1987	Web application scripting

All of these languages are flexible enough to be used to create software for many kinds of things, but usually one language has an advantage over another in certain areas. For example, assembly language is great for making software that's small and fast, but it's not easy to master. C is almost as good as assembly language for many of the same sort of things, and it's much better than assembly if you need to move your code from one kind of machine to another (this quality is called portability). LISP and Smalltalk are great for fancy, mindbending software (programs that reason about themselves!). Forth is good for controlling machinery (Forth is the programming language that flies NASA's Space Shuttle). Java is good for programming application servers (I know you're wondering what that means). There are so many languages, some for special purposes.

A Short History of BASIC

In 1964 at the Dartmouth College, John G. Kemeny and Thomas E. Kurtz wanted a programming language that would be easy to learn. They created BASIC (Beginner's All-purpose Symbolic Instruction Code). Most languages were compilers, but BASIC was an interpreter. This meant that instead of submitting a whole program in one shot (compilers work this way), the programmer could type code in a line at a time and try running the program at any moment. More code could be added or changed pretty much instantly. This mattered much more in those days because computers were much slower. Running a compiler for even a simple program was frustrating. BASIC eliminated the long delays of compiling, and this made it easier to learn because it was quicker for a beginner to recover from mistakes, and much easier (and more fun) to experiment. BASIC was a hit!

In the 1970's Bill Gates and Paul Allen founded Microsoft selling the BASIC interpreters they wrote for early home computers like the Altair, the Apple II, the Commodore PET, and more! BASIC was easy to learn and perfect for the small memory size of these computers, and it became the most popular first programming language for many people. There were so many different kinds of home computers, all very much different from each other, and most of them came with BASIC built right in. All you needed to do was take the computer home, plug it into your television set, turn it on, and voila! you would see something like:

```
Mega BASIC v1.03 copyright 1980 Itty Bitty Soft
47364 bytes free
Ready
>_
```

You could start writing a BASIC program right at that moment! This was a programming language for the masses. [Editors note - "In fact you couldn't hardly do anything on early computers unless you programmed them yourself."]

Microsoft's influence on BASIC became probably the strongest of all. There is a specification for a standard called ANSI BASIC, but Microsoft BASIC became *the* defacto standard. QBasic was their ultimate culmination of BASIC and many books were written to teach how to program in it. This was followed by Visual Basic. Some say this new language differs so strongly from the classic language that it isn't BASIC, but something altogether new.

Introducing Liberty BASIC

In 1990 when Microsoft Windows finally made it in the big time with v3.0, it didn't come with new computers. You needed to pay $200 for the software. It didn't come with a version of BASIC, so you had to buy Windows software from someone else for hundreds or thousands of dollars. In 1992 the first version of Liberty BASIC appeared! Liberty BASIC was designed to be the kind of BASIC that came with home computers so that the average user could do their own programming. Over the years Liberty BASIC has been expanded and enhanced. The current version as of this writing is Liberty BASIC v4.03. This is the version of BASIC we are going to teach you in this course.

Downloading and Installing Liberty BASIC

If you haven't already installed Liberty BASIC in your computer, please take the time to do so now. If you need to download a copy, visit http://www.libertybasic.com/download.html

Making an Impression

In any computer programming language, the first thing that most students learn is to write a program called Hello World! All this program does is display the phrase "Hello World!" on the screen. In some programming languages this can require a considerable amount of work to write.

The PRINT Command

Let's write a Hello World! program in Liberty BASIC now. Start up the Liberty BASIC software. Click on the File menu and select New File. You should have a clear text editing area, like so:

Type the following line of code into the editor exactly.

```
print "Hello World!"
```

Be careful to type this exactly. For example the quotes are double quotation marks, not apostrophes. Let's run this program now. Click on the Run menu and select Run (the first item on the menu). A new window will pop up that looks something like this:

10

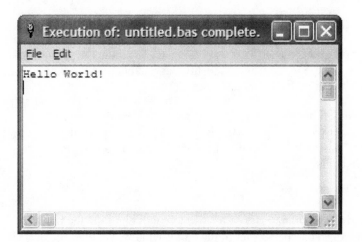

You just wrote your first Liberty BASIC program. One line of code is all it took. You just can't write a program in fewer lines than that! In Liberty BASIC parlance, the window it printed Hello World! in is called the main window (this sort of window could also be called a console).

Look at the title text at the top of the window. It says: Execution of: untitled.bas complete. This means the program has finished running. Let's close this window now by pressing Alt+F4 or by clicking on the red X button.

The command we used to make the computer display Hello World is called PRINT. Just like a mechanical printing press, the PRINT command makes an impression, but not with ink. PRINT publishes to the screen. We can use the PRINT command to display more things. Let's add a second line of code to our program. The whole program should look like this:

```
print "Hello World!"
print "And it was good!"
```

I bet you can guess what this program does. Try running it now. It displays this text:

```
Hello World!
And it was good!
```

What did you say? Why is the PRINT command in our program in lowercase letters, but I keep talking in uppercase? Liberty BASIC can actually understand commands in uppercase or lowercase, but for clarity, I use uppercase letters for commands in my text. If you're curious, try changing `print` to `PRINT` and run the program again.

Let's save our program to your hard disk drive. Click on the File menu and select Save As... Type in the name goodstuff.bas and click on the Save button. Now we can go back to it any time.

Before we go any further, let's type in a mistake. Yes, really. I want to show what happens when Liberty BASIC tries to run a program that has a mistake in it. Change the first line by removing the first quotation mark so that it looks like this:

```
print Hello World!"
```

Now try to run the program. The editor window will highlight the line with the mistake, and at the bottom of the editor window you will see *BASIC Compile Halted: Syntax error.* A syntax error happens when the format of some BASIC code has a mistake in it, so Liberty BASIC stops to show where it is so you can fix it. Sometimes the specific error might not be a syntax error, but that's okay. Just look at the highlighted line in the editor and see if you can find the mistake. Then fix it, and try to run again.

Now let's put the quotation mark back in before we continue so that it looks like this:

```
print "Hello World!"
```

The NOTICE Command (also known as PRINT-with-*zing*)

The PRINT command is a feature of the earliest versions of BASIC. You can see that it is good for displaying information on the screen, sort of like it would appear if keyed into a typewriter. While this is all you need for some kinds of software, it is rather old fashioned. [Editor's note - Boring in other words]

Oh PRINT command, where is thy *zing*?

What is *zing* you ask? My dictionary defines *zing* as "an enjoyably exciting or stimulating quality".

Let's add *zing* now. To do this, edit our goodstuff.bas program text so that

12

it looks like this:

```
notice "Hello World!"
print "And it was good!"
```

See how we replaced the PRINT command with a NOTICE command? This is how we bring our Hello World! program into the modern age. Try running it now.

Tada! - *a sound plays and you see this pop up!*

The NOTICE command adds some sound and animation to our little program. Cool! Click on okay, and you'll see that it still executed the PRINT command:

```
And it was good!
```

What do you think would happen if we also changed the second PRINT command to a NOTICE command? Change it now and run the program, then save this new version of the Hello World! program as zing.bas.

Performing Math

Now that we've seen a couple of ways to display text messages, let's explore how to use BASIC to do what computers are supposed to be really good at... math.

Let's make a little program that adds two numbers together. Once again, make a new file by clicking on Liberty BASIC's File menu and select New File. Type in this short program:

```
print "The world's biggest pocket calculator says..."
print 3+4
```

Can you guess what this program does? Run it now. You should see this:

```
The world's biggest pocket calculator says...
7
```

See how the second PRINT command in our program causes the value of
3+4 to be computed and displayed? You may also have noticed that there
are no quotation marks around the 3+4. This is Liberty BASIC's clue that
it should consider what's after the PRINT command as something to be
computed. Save the program with the filename seven.bas, then try
changing the second line to the following and run the program again:

```
print "3+4"
```

Did it display what you expected? The quotation marks tell the PRINT
command to display what's in between *exactly* as it appears. This is just
like when you see a famous person quoted. It means they said these exact
words. "Imagination is more important than knowledge..." -- Albert
Einstein

This will prove to be useful, but let's get back to math.

Let's modify our program so that it looks like this:

```
print "The world's biggest pocket calculator says..."
print 3+4*5
```

What's that funny * character for? This doesn't look like any math they
teach in school, right? The mystery symbol * (an asterisk) is used for
multiplying numbers. This isn't just in BASIC, but most programming
languages use * for multiplication. Perhaps programming languages could
use the letter x for multiplication (which would look like print 3+4x5),
but this is actually harder than it seems for reasons we'll have to explain
later on.

Try running this program. Does it give you the answer you expected? On
my computer it ran like this:

```
The world's biggest pocket calculator says...
23
```

Surprised? This really is the right answer. When Liberty BASIC
calculates, it follows the rules of *arithmetic precedence*. This means that
some math operations take place before others. Multiplication comes
before addition, so first 4*5 is computed to be 20, and then the 3 and 20
are added to make 23. You can change the order if you need to by using

14

parenthesis. Try this example:

```
print "The world's biggest pocket calculator says..."
print (3+4)*5
```

Here's the result:

```
The world's biggest pocket calculator says...
35
```

This time 3 and 4 are added, resulting in the number 7. The 7 and 5 are multiplied to make 35.

Here are some different operations. Their order in this list reflects their place in the rules of *arithmetic precedence*, first to last:

Operators	Name	Example
^	raise to a power	`print 5^7`
*, /	multiply, divide	`print 10*6/3`
+, -	add, subtract	`print 4+5-9`

You'll notice that multiplication and division share the same position in *arithmetic precedence*. Addition and subtract also share the same position. Let's try one more, fancier computation:

```
print "My expensive pocket calculator earned its pay"
print 2*3+4^3/5
```

Okay, before we run this, let's step into the computer's shoes and try to predict what answer it will give us.

Starting with: 2*3+4^3/5

First, we raise to a power, so $4\wedge3 = 4 * 4 * 4 = 64$

Our expression becomes:2*3+64/5

Second, we do the multiplication and division, so $2 * 3 = 6$ and $64 / 5 = 12.8$

Our expression becomes:6+12.8

Third, we do the addition, so $6+12.8 = 18.8$

Let's run the program to check our answer:

```
My expensive pocket calculator earned its pay
18.8
```

String and Numeric Literals

Let's stop for a moment to introduce a simple idea with a fancy name. All programming languages let you type values right into the code in your programs. For example:

```
print "The world's biggest pocket calculator says..."
print 3+4*5
```

In the first line we see a *string literal*. This starts with the first quotation mark, and ends at the second quotation mark.

```
"The world's biggest pocket calculator says..."
```

It is called a *literal* because you can read it by looking at the program code. It isn't some mysterious computed value that you never get to see. Why do they call it a string? *Whoa, hold on! I hope there aren't any strings in my computer, all tangled up in there. I'm almost afraid to open my eyes.*
Don't worry, it's nothing like that. It's called a string because it is a bunch of characters (letters, numbers and other symbols) all connected in a row. In other words, a *string* of characters. Of course there are also threads in your computer, errr... Never mind, different programming language. ;-)

Okay, so that's a string literal. Let's look at the second line of code. Can you see the *numeric literals*? That's right. The 3, and the 4 and the 5 are all numeric literals. You can read them right in the code.

Exercise: Ask your english teacher if you can get extra credit for reading string literals. ;-)

16

Thinking Green with PRINT

Let's have a look at some useful things you can do with PRINT. Let's have a look at the seven.bas program we wrote earlier. Click on the File menu, select Open... and click on the file named seven.bas. Now click the Open button.

```
print "The world's biggest pocket calculator says..."
print 3+4
```

In this day and age, we want to conserve natural resources. Think green, right? This little gem of a program displays two lines of information when you run it, but we want it to display everything on just one line to save screen space. How green would that be?! Right on! BASIC has got it covered using the ; character (a semicolon). If you're like me, you never much liked semicolons, but don't worry about it. This is easy. Modify your program by adding a semicolon to the end of the first line. It should look like this:

```
print "The world's biggest pocket calculator says...";
print 3+4
```

The first PRINT command displays the string literal, just as before. The PRINT command also notices the semicolon on the end of the line. Usually the PRINT command will put the display cursor to the beginning of the next line, but not when your PRINT line ends in a semicolon. Instead, it leaves the display cursor right there at the end of the line without going to the next line. The next PRINT command will then make its mark starting at the end of that line. Try running the program now.

```
The world's biggest pocket calculator says...7
```

Now we're not wasting so much screen space! How about that? Not green enough? There's more! We can save even more screen space by making our program code shorter. How do we do this? It's that semicolon again! Delete the second line of the program and modify the first line to look like this:

```
print "The world's biggest pocket calculator says..."; 3+4
```

Our little program is now even smaller. Now we're back to one line of code again! The PRINT command sees the semicolon and displays the string literal in front of it, then the computation of 3+4 is performed and

17

PRINT displays the result on the same line. Run it now and you'll see:

```
The world's biggest pocket calculator says...7
```

It's Not Easy Being Green - LPRINT

Now that we've figured out how to save screen space, we're going to show you how to consume paper. Sorry about this, but it's part of the lesson, okay?

If you want to print out the answer to 3+4, you'll be glad to know it's really, really easy. Liberty BASIC includes a special version of the PRINT command, called LPRINT. I know, maybe it should be called PAPERPRINT, or something like that, but LPRINT is the standard name for the command.

Change our one line program to look like this:

```
lprint "The world's biggest pocket calculator says..."; 3+4
```

That looks just like the PRINT command! That's easy. Actually we aren't done yet. When a PRINT command displays on the screen, it doesn't wait for anything. In some of our programs we have two PRINT commands. The first one just displays immediately right on the screen, and then the second one does the same. LPRINT can't do the same thing. We don't want to immediately print out a sheet of paper when LPRINT does its thing. There might be more stuff to print on the page, right? We don't want to waste paper, so instead, LPRINT stores up the stuff it will put on paper. This is called buffering. We have a special command that takes all that buffered text and prints it all at once onto a sheet (or more) of paper. This command is called DUMP.

Here is what our complete program looks like:

```
lprint "The world's biggest pocket calculator says..."; 3+4
dump
```

When you run this, the program will send its output to your printer. Now you have something to put in the recycle bin. The program's main window will not have anything in it.

18

Quiz - Answers on the next page

1) BASIC is an acronym for

_____.

2) The official standard for BASIC is called _____

_____.

3) The defacto standard for BASIC is _____ _____.

4) The name of the command for displaying information on screen is

_____.

5) A string or numeric literal gets its name because you can
_____ it.

6) A syntax error happens when you try to run a program with a
_____ in it.

7) A fancier way than the PRINT command for displaying information is
the _____ command.

8) The rules that control the order in which math operators evaluate are
called _____.

9) More than one thing can be displayed on a line by using a
_____ with the PRINT command.

10) The LPRINT command stores up what is to be printed using a
technique called _____.

11) The _____ command causes text buffered by the LPRINT
command to be printed on paper.

12) The PRINT command sends text to the _____.

Answers

1) Beginner's All-Purpose Symbolic Instruction Code

2) ANSI BASIC

3) Microsoft BASIC

4) PRINT

5) read

6) mistake

7) NOTICE

8) arithmetic precedence

9) semicolon

10) buffering

11) DUMP

12) main window

Chapter Two

Juggling information

In our first lesson we showed some ways to display information using the PRINT, NOTICE, LPRINT and DUMP commands. We wrote small programs using string and numeric literals to display text and numbers and to compute some numeric values. Because these program's string and numeric literals are always the same, the programs always do the same thing every time they are run. Imagine using a phone that has only one button (a Run button?). While this might be better than no phone at all, I'm glad that I can dial billions of different phone numbers. We can write programs that can do billions of things, and in this lesson we'll show how to begin.

Variables

Let's take again the example of a phone. When I pick up the phone to call my mother, is the phone different somehow than when I use it to call my tax accountant? Well, no. What makes calling mom different than calling Jim? The phone number!

So, for each different person I want to call, the phone number changes. In other words, the phone number *varies*. What are some other things that change like this? Most everything changes. The weather changes. The value of your car changes. The length of your fingernails changes. Your opinion sometimes changes. Of course we can't put any of these sorts of things into a computer program, but we can put information into a computer program. Up to this point, the information we put into the computer program was in the form of string literals and numeric literals. This kind of information changes only when you are writing code. Once a program is running the values are frozen and can't be changed.

Programming languages have a name for things that change while a program runs. Things that change are called *variables*. So, just as we have string literals and numeric literals that can not change, we also have string variables and numeric variables which can change.

21

Here's a sports analogy. Let's compare a Football (American Football) game to a computer program. Let's imagine we have a big scoreboard with the following information.

> Home Team: Littlefield School Giants
> Visiting Team: McGrath School Rockets
> Offense: Home Team
> Home score: 7
> Visitor score: 0
> Line of Scrimmage: 52 yard line
> Quarter: First
> Time left: 3 mins 20 secs
> Down: Second
> Yards to go for first down: 6

Whew! That's a lot of information (and I probably forgot something important)!

While the football game goes on, the information on the scoreboard changes. When we need to know something about the game we look at the scoreboard for the information by its name. Depending on what's already on the board, the game progresses one way or the other. When we figure out that the information is changed we update the scoreboard.

It is helpful to compare a computer program to the football game. The scoreboard is like the memory of the program, holding variables. The program uses its variables to keep score, so to speak, of how things are going. It also updates the contents of its variables.

Let's have a look at a program that uses a variable. Type in the following small program. Try running it to see Tom practicing his division.

```
xyz = 4.98
print "Clerk says: Lunch costs $"; xyz
print "Tom says: You said $"; xyz/2; " for that lunch?"
end
```

This program gives a variable named xyz a value of 4.98 with the first line:

```
xyz = 4.98
```

This is called an *assignment*. The variable xyz is assigned a value of 4.98. Imagine one of those big stadium scoreboards. The only thing on the board is a great big **xyz: 0**. When the assignment happens it changes to an even bigger **xyz: 4.98**!

Now let's look at the next line:

```
print "Clerk says: Lunch costs $"; xyz
```

The PRINT command displays the string literal, and then it looks up the variable xyz on its scoreboard and finds and displays the number 4.98.

The second PRINT command displays a string literal, and then there is a math expression which includes our variable xyz. The program looks up the value of xyz and divides it by two, displaying the answer. Then it wraps up by displaying the second string literal.

```
print "Tom says: You said $"; xyz/2; " for that lunch?"
```

Finally we get to the END command and our program stops.

The xyz school of variable naming

You may be wondering why I chose the name xyz for our variable. There is a method to my madness. Take a glance at our football scoreboard again. If you know the game of football, everything on the board has a name that makes sense. Let's rehash it so that it follows **The xyz school of variable naming** method:

> abc: Littlefield School Giants
> i: McGrath School Rockets
> j: Home Team
> k: 7
> xyz: 0
> pdq: 52 yard line
> a1: First
> a2: 3 mins 20 secs
> a3: Second
> q: 6

This looks like a really bad idea, right? I stress this because a lot of people choose variable names that look just like the above. Once upon a time there were reasons to choose silly, short names for program variables. Computers had tiny memories (long variable names took up more memory), and some early BASIC interpreters only permitted the choice of variable names with 2 or 3 characters. These days computers have tons of

23

memory. Take advantage of this and choose really nice, descriptive names for your variables. Let's rename our xyz variable to something more helpful:

```
lunchPrice = 4.98
print "Clerk says: Lunch costs $"; lunchPrice
print "Tom says: You said $"; lunchPrice/2; " for that
lunch?"
end
```

That's better! The names you choose for variables (and as you'll see later, other things) matter a lot, especially if will share your code with others. Even in the professional world I sometimes still hear over the cubicle walls words like "What does this cotton pickin code do?!!" Sometimes it's the author of the code who says it. Returning to read your own code and not understanding what it does is particularly frustrating.

A carefully chosen name is sometimes called an *intention revealing* name, which is a simple and obvious idea that isn't practiced as widely as one might hope.

Let's add another intention revealing name to our program. Have a look:

```
lunchPrice = 4.98
print "Clerk says: Lunch costs $"; lunchPrice
halfPrice = lunchPrice/2
print "Tom says: You said $"; halfPrice; " for that
lunch?"
end
```

You may have noticed so far that our variables lunchPrice and halfPrice hold only numeric values. They are *numeric variables*. There are also variables that can hold string values. In BASIC we make a *string variable* by adding a $ character to the end of its name. Here is a version of our lunch example that uses a string variable.

```
lunchPrice = 4.98
print "Clerk says: Lunch costs $"; lunchPrice
halfPrice = lunchPrice/2
customerName$ = "Tom"
print customerName$;
print " says: You said $"; halfPrice; " for that lunch?"
end
```

See how the program uses the string variable customerName$ to hold the name Tom? Of course it could hold any name you would like.

24

One thing we haven't demonstrated in our examples here is of variables holding different values during a program run. Here is an example of a variable changing value:

```
summary$ = "Total count of fruit is "
bananas = 5
mangos = 3
apples = 7
totalFruit = totalFruit + bananas
totalFruit = totalFruit + mangos
totalFruit = totalFruit + apples
print summary$; totalFruit
end
```

When the program begins to run, the variables bananas, mangos, apples and totalFruit all have a value of zero right at the program's start. The summary$ variable is an empty string, or equal to "". Then we start assigning more interesting values to our variables.

When we get down to the part where we begin to calculate the value of totalFruit, each line gets the value of totalFruit and adds the count of bananas, mangos or apples. The value of totalFruit changes 3 times, from zero to 5, from 5 to 8, and from 8 to 15. Then we print it out.

Note: You can't put a string value in a numeric variable, and you can't put a numeric value in a string variable. Try the following short program. It won't run:

```
needANumber = "I'm a string."
print needANumber
end
```

When you try to run it you get a **type mismatch** error. This means that Liberty BASIC saw the program wanted to put a value of one type (string) into a variable for another type (number).

Idea Break! - Camel casing

When choosing names for variables you can choose to capitalize some letters in the name. Consider the following variations:

```
spittinganimalcounter
SPITTINGANIMALCOUNTER
spittingAnimalCounter
```

Remember that each of these is a unique variable name in Liberty BASIC (some BASIC languages treat them as the same variable).

Lowercase letters are proven to be easier for the brain to read than uppercase letters, but many traditional BASIC programmers seem to prefer all uppercase letters.

The third example is the easiest of all to read. Starting with the second word in the variable name, the first letter of each word is capitalized. This kind of capitalization is called camel casing because it makes for variable names that look like they have camel humps. :-)

INPUT and PROMPT

Now let's go back to our phone analogy. We wanted to make a phone that could dial more than one number. Now that we have variables, we should be able to do this, right? Here's a simulation of a phone call:

```
print "Please enter a phone number to dial."
phoneNumber$ = "1-435-223-1110"
print "Now dialing "; phoneNumber$
print "Phone rings a couple of times..."
print "The number you have dialed... "; phoneNumber$
print "is not in service.  Please try again."
```

If my eyes do not deceive me, this is a (cheap) simulation of a phone that only dials one number. You actually have to edit the program to dial a different number! This is like making a whole new phone just to dial a different number. If picking up the phone is the equivalent of running the program, then we need a command that will let us make a change to the program *after* it starts to run. This command is called INPUT.

All we have to do is replace the assignment statement for the variable

26

phoneNumber$. Here is the new program:

```
print "Please enter a phone number to dial."
input phoneNumber$
print "Now dialing "; phoneNumber$
print "Phone rings a couple of times..."
print "The number you have dialed... "; phoneNumber$
print "is not in service.  Please try again."
```

When you run this program it will stop and ask you to type a phone number. This is the INPUT command in action. Type in a phone number and press Enter. Whatever phone number you put in, the INPUT command will assign the string you type to the variable phoneNumber$. Then the program will (pretend to) dial that number. ;-)

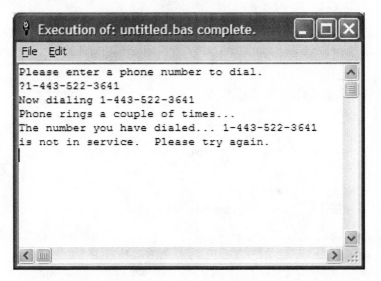

If we wanted to write a program that really does dial a phone number for us, it can be done. To do this we need a modem and a little more know-how. This simple program only pretends to dial a phone, and it always tells you the number is out of service.

You can use the INPUT command to get strings and numbers from the user when a program is running. Here is a simple adding calculator. Try running it.

```
print "Enter a number."
input firstNumber
print "Enter another number."
```

27

```
input secondNumber
print "The sum of these two numbers is:"
print firstNumber + secondNumber
end
```

Now run it again, entering data that are not numbers. What happens? If the INPUT command is servicing a numeric variable and you type something non-numeric, this will generally result in a zero assignment to that variable.

The INPUT command also has a format which combines a PRINT command functionality. You can display some instructions with the INPUT command like so:

```
input "What is your name?"; yourName$
```

It looks like a PRINT command, but it isn't. It displays What is your name? and then stops and waits for you to type something and press Enter.

We can rewrite our adding calculator using this new form of INPUT:

```
input "Enter a number?"; firstNumber
input "Enter another number?"; secondNumber
print "The sum of these two numbers is:"
print firstNumber + secondNumber
end
```

PROMPT - INPUT's pop-up cousin

Remember the command NOTICE, the pop-up version of PRINT? There is also a pop-up version of INPUT called PROMPT. In code, PROMPT looks almost just like INPUT. Here's a version of our adding calculator that uses PROMPT. For good measure, let's use the NOTICE command too!

```
prompt "Enter a number?"; firstNumber
prompt "Enter another number?"; secondNumber
notice "The sum of these two numbers is:"
notice firstNumber + secondNumber
end
```

Run it now. It works, but it's annoying, right? I call this kind of programming Whack-a-Mole style, after the arcade machine where you hit moles over the head when they pop up. It's good to know how to pop up

28

notices and prompts, but it's also good to be careful not to overuse these features.

Idea Break! - Functions

Most programming language have some built in capabilities for getting a value from some other value. These are usually called functions. This is different from a PRINT statement for example because PRINT doesn't return a value.

Here is a simple example of a function in action:

```
myWord$ = word$("I'm the third word", 3)
```

In this case the WORD$( ) function takes two values (the string "I'm the third word", and the number 3), and it returns the string "third". We assign that returned value to the myWord$ variable.

Liberty BASIC comes with a bunch of built-in functions (called *intrinsic functions*), and you can also define your own, which we will cover later in the book.

Things you can do, especially with strings

When writing software, we seldom leave well enough alone. To accomplish this goal we invent all kinds of ways for doing stuff to numbers and strings. We push them around, pick them up, drop them, kick them, cut them up, paste them back together, and more! Hey, it's all in a day's work!

String concatenation (adding strings together) - In BASIC you can make one string out of two or more strings by using +. This doesn't perform math on the strings (and you can't use *, /, or - with strings), but it just joins them together to make a longer string. This is called concatenation. What do you think the following program does?

29

```
print "Let's conjugate a verb."
adding$ = "add" + "ing"
print adding$
end
```

Here's another example:

```
input "What is your first name?"; firstName$
input "What is your last name?"; lastName$
fullName$ = firstName$ + " " + lastName$
print "Nice to meet you, "; fullName$
end
```

The WORDS( ) function - This neat function (a function is a kind of command) let's you say "Give me the word I want from this string." Here's an example:

```
quip$ = "The quick brown fox jumped over the lazy dog."
input "Which word do you want (enter a number)?"; index
wantedWord$ = word$(quip$, index)
print "The word is: "; wantedWord$
end
```

Run the program. If you type 1, you'll get the word The. What word do you get if you type 6? What word do you get if you type 20? You don't get any word at all, but an empty string "" because there are only 8 words in the string.

The VAL( ) and STR$( ) functions - Sometimes we need to convert a string to a number, or a number to a string.

The VAL( ) function converts a string to a number. Here is an example:

```
piString$ = "3.14"
print "Sorry string, but I need a number."
piNumber = val(piString$)
print "Pi times two is: "; piNumber * 2
end
```

Well, one good turn deserves another, so let's be fair to the string:

```
areaCode = 301
exchange = 620
last4Digits = 2421
phoneNumber$ = phoneNumber$ + str$(areaCode)
phoneNumber$ = phoneNumber$ + "-" + str$(exchange)
phoneNumber$ = phoneNumber$ + "-" + str$(last4Digits)
print "The phone number is: "; phoneNumber$
print "No, I didn't just make it up!  ;-)"
end
```

Using the debugger

As you develop your programs and they get bigger and more complicated it can become difficult to get a sense for what's going on. For example if a program isn't doing what you expect you might wonder if the variables are being assigned the values you intend. It would be nice to be able to see how things change as the program runs so that you can change it to work the way it should.

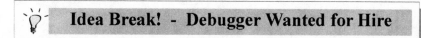
Idea Break! - Debugger Wanted for Hire

Way back when computers were based on vacuum tubes (yes, they were!) they were so big that computers filled whole buildings. There were rooms containing isles of racks of logic circuits made of tubes.

The tubes would burn out frequently. When this happened the computer would exhibit a bug. This is not the same as a bug in a program, but an actual bug in the computer itself.

To keep the computer working correctly there was a runner whose only job was to tour the inside of the computer to look for bad tubes and replace them. Imagine that. A human debugger! In the Winter this was probably a nice job, but I'd hate to do that in the heat of Summer!

Liberty BASIC has a special tool that lets you look inside the program while it runs. You can see which part of code is about to be executed, and you also get the see the scoreboard of variables and watch them change. This tool is called a debugger. It helps you to debug your programs. It's also really good as a learning tool, so we can "see the computer think."

Let's try the debugger out on the program above. To start it up, click on the run menu and select the option Debug. You will see a window that looks like this:

```
Debugging - Debugging                                    _ □ ×
Code  File  Edit

▷  ‖   ⟫  ↻  ⟲  ⟫⟫  ❷

areaCode    = 0                                              ▲
exchange    = 0
last4Digits = 0
phoneNumber$ = ""                                           ▼

                                              ▼    Execute

☐ On top      ☐ Manually scroll variables    ☐ Show default variables

 areaCode = 301                                             ▲
 exchange = 620
 last4Digits = 2421
 phoneNumber$ = phoneNumber$ + str$(areaCode)
 phoneNumber$ = phoneNumber$ + "-" + str$(exchange)
 phoneNumber$ = phoneNumber$ + "-" + str$(last4Digits)
 print "The phone number is: "; phoneNumber$
 print "No, I didn't just make it up!  ;-)"
 end
                                                            ▼
◄ ▓                                                      ►
```

Move and resize the debugger so you can also see the program's main window.

See the list of variables at the top of the debugger? The numeric variables are all zero, and the string variable phoneNumber$ is an empty string. This is the way all variables start out (there are special cases though, which you'll learn about later). In the code listing below, the first line is highlighted. This means Liberty BASIC is ready to execute that line.

Let's step through the program. Look for the button that looks like this:

This is called the Step button. Click on that button once. See how the value of the variable areaCode changed? Also, the next line of code is selected, ready to be executed.

32

Code File Edit

```
areaCode      = 301
exchange      = 0
last4Digits   = 0
phoneNumber$ = ""
```

[   ] [Execute]

☐ On top   ☐ Manually scroll variables   ☐ Show default variables

```
   areaCode = 301
   exchange = 620
   last4Digits = 2421
   phoneNumber$ = phoneNumber$ + str$(areaCode)
   phoneNumber$ = phoneNumber$ + "-" + str$(exchange)
   phoneNumber$ = phoneNumber$ + "-" + str$(last4Digits)
   print "The phone number is: "; phoneNumber$
   print "No, I didn't just make it up!  ;-)"
   end
```

12:17:50 : Stepped over

Click on the Step button again and again, studying how the variables change. When you get down to the PRINT commands, notice how they output to main window. When you're all done you can close the debugger or the main window. Both windows will close.

Now let's debug a program with an INPUT command. This requires a little special instruction.

```
print "Enter a number."
input firstNumber
print "Enter another number."
input secondNumber
print "The sum of these two numbers is:"
print firstNumber + secondNumber
end
```

Start the debugger. Click on the Step button and the INPUT command will be highlighted. You'll need to click on the Step button again to execute the INPUT command. Then, you must enter something into the main window and press Enter before you can Step again in the debugger.

We will cover more on the debugger in future lessons. This is a great tool. Use it often to get a feel for how programs really work!

33

Exercises

1) Scoreboard Program - Take the football scoreboard we showed in the beginning of the lesson (reproduced below) and write a program that duplicates the information into appropriately named string and numeric variables, and then prints them out to the main window:

> Home Team: Littlefield School Giants
> Visiting Team: McGrath School Rockets
> Offense: Home Team
> Home score: 7
> Visitor score: 0
> Line of Scrimmage: 52 yard line
> Quarter: First
> Time left: 3 mins 20 secs
> Down: Second
> Yards to go for first down: 6

2) Mad Libs Game - Write a short program that asks the user for each part of speech in parenthesis below, then outputs the text complete with the words the user typed in. The example below is credited to Papa English (no copyright).

> A Day at the Zoo
>
> Today I went to the zoo. I saw a *(adjective)* *(noun)* jumping up and down in its tree. He *(verb: past tense)* *(adverb)* through the large tunnel that led to its *(adjective) (noun)*. I got some peanuts and passed them through the cage to a gigantic gray *(noun)* towering above my head. Feeding that *(noun)* made me *(adjective)*. I went to get a *(adjective)* scoop of ice cream. It *(verb: past tense)* my stomach. Afterwards I had to *(verb) (adverb)* to catch our bus. When I got home I *(verb past tense)* my mom for a *(adjective)* day at the zoo.

Quiz - Answers on the next page

1) A _____ holds information that changes.

2) A numeric variable holds a number value, and a string variable holds a _____ _____.

3) The word used to describe giving a value to a variable is _____.

4) Names for string variables must end with a _____ character.

5) The command used to ask the user for some information is called _____.

6) The pop-up command for getting information is called _____.

7) Joining two or more strings together is called _____.

8) If you try to put a string into a numeric variable you get a _____ _____ error.

9) Converting strings to numbers is done with the _____ function.

10) Converting numbers to strings is done with the _____ function.

11) The careful naming of a variable is known as _____ revealing

12) _____ casing is the style of capitalization where the first letter of each word in a variable name is uppercased.

Answers

1) variable

2) string value

3) assignment

4) $

5) INPUT

6) PROMPT

7) concatenation

8) type mismatch

9) VAL( )

10) STR$( )

11) intention

12) camel

Chapter Three
Decisions, decisions!

The programs we have written so far do what they do only once. Each time you want to use our handy little programs you need to run them again from the start. This can get to be tedious and even error prone (say rubber baby buggy bumpers ten times fast). What we need is a way for our program to go to the beginning and do it over. In BASIC the command for doing this is called GOTO (surprise!).

Knowing that we have to go to some place is not enough. We also need to know where to go. When you hop into your car in a foreign country looking for a food market, you at least know what you are looking for. Liberty BASIC can't ask for directions, so you need to be very precise. Fasten your safety belt because we're about to take a high speed tour!

GOTO and branch labels

The mechanism that Liberty BASIC uses to mark places that we can GOTO is called a branch label. This is a lot like an address. When you send someone on an errand, they need one or more addresses. The errand runner goes to some place and there is something to do there. So in the same way, you mark the place in your BASIC program where you want it to continue running with a branch label (an address of sorts).

Here is a short example of a program that uses a branch label:

```
[startOver]
  print "What is your name?"
  input yourName$
  print yourName$; "! Whoa! Deja vu! "
  goto [startOver]
  end
```

Can you spot the branch label? It's the only thing you see in the first line of code, and it's used later on in the GOTO command.

The branch label is:

```
[startOver]
```

Try running the program. What does it do? When we are finished with it, we can close it like any other Windows program by double-clicking on the system menu box. Now try stepping through the program in the debugger.

As you can see, when the program executes the GOTO command, it goes back to the code immediately following the branch label, and continues running there. When a computer program executes the same code over and over in this way, this is called a *loop*. Since there is no way to stop the looping (short of shutting down the program), this is called an *infinite loop*. This isn't usually very useful in and of itself. We actually wrote an infinite loop on purpose, but usually these things happen by mistake, and they result in a program hanging (like when your CD player gets stuck and repeats the same half a second of music over and over).

Here are some more examples of branch labels:

    [start.over] [loopBack] [getResponse] [point1] etc...

They look a lot like variable names, but they start and end with square braces.

Examples of unacceptable branch labels:

    [loop back]   no spaces allowed
    start   must use brackets
    (point1)   only use square brackets

Since no spaces are allowed in the alphanumeric branch labels, it works well to capitalize the first letter in each word when multiple words are used in a branch label. For example [gettimedresponse] is valid, but [getTimedResponse] is much more readable (remember camel case from the last chapter?). Periods can also be used, so [get.timed.response] is also ok.

Decisions, decisions...

Ah, now we get down to it! Now that we have learned to make a program smart enough to do something more than once, we are now compelled to make it even smarter. The program must decide when to stop looping.

The IF THEN command

The IF THEN command is a direct descendant of those do-it-yourself style instruction manual texts. For example:

Problem: Your car's engine won't turn over
1) Check your battery for correct voltage.
2) If voltage is less than 11 volts then goto to step 13
3) Clean and tighten ground connection.
4) If this doesn't solve the trouble, continue to step 5.
5) Remove the starter.
6) Connect starter directly to battery
7) If starter does not spin then goto step 18
8) Check starter relay.
. . .
13) Charge battery
. . .
18) See chapter 4 on rebuilding the starter unit

Notice how in the above example how you are led smartly through the troubleshooting procedure. The steps containing the words *if* and *then* make it possible to work through a complex procedure. In the same way, the IF THEN command in BASIC makes it possible to add a kind of intelligence to your programs.

Let's apply this idea directly to our example program from the previous section. Run this program and then step through it in the debugger:

```
[startOver]
  print "What is your name?"
  input yourName$
  if yourName$ = "" then goto [nothingEntered]
  print yourName$; "!  Whoa!  Deja vu! "
  goto [startOver]
[nothingEntered]
  print "What?  Cat got your tongue?  Bye!"
  end
```

Now we have two branch labels. The [startOver] branch label is still used to go back and ask for another name, but the new branch label [nothingEntered] is where we go when the user of the program presses Enter without first entering a name.

The really new and interesting thing is this line:

```
if yourName$ = "" then goto [nothingEntered]
```

This line of code does exactly how it reads. *If the string variable yourName$ is equal to an empty string, then GOTO [nothingEntered].* If the user of the program presses Enter without typing anything, the value of yourName$ is set to "", and the rest is automatic. After saying goodbye, the program ends.

In our first short program, we had a simple infinite loop. Our IF THEN statement makes it possible to stop looping. This is called *breaking out* of a loop.

IF THEN is a very versatile command. Here is a short program that uses IF THEN to make the loop happen instead of using it to break out of a loop. Can you guess what this program does? Run this program and then step through it in the debugger:

```
  print "L";
[oneMoreTime]
  print "OO";
  counter = counter + 1
  if counter < 10 then goto [oneMoreTime]
  print "PY!"
  end
```

First we display the letter L. Then we enter the [oneMoreTime] loop. Each time the code in this loop executes it displays a two letter O's and it adds the value 1 to the numeric variable counter. Each time the IF THEN command executes, it tests to see if counter is less than 10. If counter is less than 10 then we loop back and repeat. Eventually counter will be 10, the IF THEN test will fail, and we finish up by displaying PY!.

It is all too easy to mistakenly write code that loops with no way out. For example:

```
  print "L";
[oneMoreTime]
  print "OO";
  counter = counter + 1
  if count < 10 then goto [oneMoreTime]
  print "PY!"
  end
```

This will loop forever unless we stop it because we mispelled counter in the IF/THEN statement. See how it says count instead? The value of count will always be zero. This program will run on and one. Not only will it loop forever, but it will keep printing "OO". This consumes more and more memory. This is a kind of *memory leak*.

How do stop such runaway code? Press Ctrl-Break.

Less is More

Okay, now that we've seen IF THEN used to compare both strings and numbers, let's take a little detour and look at this in a little more detail. Here is a list of the *comparison operators*.

```
a = b      a is equal to b
a <> b     a is unequal to b
a < b      a is less than b
a > b      a is greater than b
a <= b     a is less than or equal to b
a >= b     a is greater than or equal to b
```

These operators work for strings and and they work for numbers, but differently. According to the operator you choose, the item on the left is tested against the item on the right, and the result is either true or false.

For numeric values the comparison operators work more or less the way you might expect. For example:

```
  if 5 < 6 then goto [fiveIsLessThanSix]
```

This line of code has no surprises. It does what you expect it to.

Now for strings. Consider the following line:

```
if "Ice" = "Cream" then print "I scream"
```

This line also does what you expect. The word Ice and the word Cream are not the same, so if you test to see if they are equal, you will get a result of false. The `print "I scream"` would not be executed.

How about the following? Are they different?

```
if "Basic" <> "BASIC" then print "Not the same."
```

Yup. They're different. To be equal, they have to be **exactly** the same.

Where string comparisons get interesting is when you start testing strings to see if one is greater or less than another. In grade school we all learn to sort words alphabetically. This is an important skill if you want to find words in a dictionary.

Let's take a stab at a string comparison:

```
if "blue" < "red" then print "blue comes before red."
```

No surprise there. All is well in the world. ;-) Not so fast...

```
if "Red" < "blue" then print "Red comes before blue."
```

No, there's no typo in this code. In this reality, Red really does come before blue (*wake up, the matrix has you!*). The answer lays in the uppercase R. The reason why is a little esoteric, but in a nutshell it's because most programming languages compare and sort strings *alphanumerically* instead of alphabetically.

Under the covers every numeric, alphabetic and other symbol you can type in or read on the screen is given a unique numeric value, known as an *ASCII value* (in internationalized software it is even more complicated, but we won't go down that rabbit hole now). Each letter has an upper and lower case, and each case of a letter has it's own unique numeric value. Uppercase letters A to Z have ASCII values 65 to 90, and lowercase letters a to z have ASCII values 97 to 122.

It becomes a simple numbers game. The uppercase letter R has an ASCII value of 82, but the letter b which comes before R in the alphabet has an

ASCII value of 98. So clearly R is less than b, don't you think? It's not such a hard pill to swallow after all.

Building with blocks

I could speak metaphorically about building software out of blocks, but I don't need to. There really are things called blocks in programming languages. In Liberty BASIC, they're used with the IF THEN command. Consider this program we wrote earlier in the lesson:

```
[startOver]
  print "What is your name?"
  input yourName$
  if yourName$ = "" then goto [nothingEntered]
  print yourName$; "!  Whoa!  Deja vu! "
  goto [startOver]
[nothingEntered]
  print "What?  Cat got your tongue?  Bye!"
  end
```

And now look at this rewrite:

```
[startOver]
  print "What is your name?"
  input yourName$
  if yourName$ <> "" then
    print yourName$; "!  Whoa!  Deja vu! "
    goto [startOver]
  end if
  print "What?  Cat got your tongue?  Bye!"
  end
```

This version of the program uses an *IF THEN block*. If the comparison is true, the code between the IF THEN command and the next END IF gets executed (END IF is not to be confused with plain END). If the comparison is false then Liberty BASIC skips right past the END IF and continues executing there. The indenting of the code inside the IF THEN block isn't required, but is commonly added by programmers for readability. Make a point of indenting your code so your code will be easier to understand.

Note: Don't miss that we replaced the = operator with the <> operator to make this change work.

44

One interesting feature of using an IF THEN block is that we eliminated a branch label and also a GOTO command from the program. This is considered good practice, to minimize the use of GOTO. When programs get large, too much jumping around with GOTO can cause confusion, and making it easy for bugs to slip into the code.

Let's try another football example by creating a first down calculator. We will show how take IF THEN blocks a step further by introducing the ELSE command.

We need to know:

- What down is it?
- How many yards to go for first down?
- How many yards did the offense advance?

With this information we will compute what down it is, and whether the ball turns over. We won't bother with trying to figure out if there was a touchdown or anything else in this example.

Okay, let's write the first part of the program that gets the information:

```
print "First Down Calculator"
input "What down is it (1, 2, 3, or 4)?"; down
input "Yards to go for 1st down?"; yardsToGo
input "Yards advanced?"; yardsAdvanced
```

Now let's get to the computational part. We need to first figure out if the yards advanced is enough for a first down:

```
if yardsAdvanced >= yardsToGo then
    down = 1
    print "First down!"
else
```

This is pretty straightforward. If we have advanced at least the number of yardsToGo, we get a first down! Where this is different from the IF THEN block we saw earlier is that it ends with ELSE rather than with END IF. This is a way to end the first block and start another block (an ELSE block) at the same time! So right after ELSE we add a block of code to compute what happens if we don't advance enough yards. Here's a more complete example (which includes the code above):

45

```
if yardsAdvanced >= yardsToGo then
    down = 1
    print "First down!"
else
    down = down + 1
    if down > 4 then
        down = 1
        print "Ball changes sides!"
    end if
    print "New down is: "; down
end if
```

Whew! Didn't I say we were going for a high speed tour? After the ELSE we put the block of code we want to execute, wrapping it up with an END IF. We didn't stop there! Notice the IF THEN block inside the ELSE block? When you put a block inside a block, this is called a *nested block*. Just to make it clear, what follows is the IF THEN block that is nested inside the ELSE block:

```
if down > 4 then
    down = 1
    print "Ball changes sides!"
end if
```

Notice how this style of coding makes it clear what part of the program belongs to another? This is one of the techniques of *structured programming*. The idea is that software should be built so that it is modular. As much as it can, each part of a program should stand alone without knowing too much about other parts of the program.

Writing modular code is something that somes with lots of practice. The use of IF THEN blocks is just an introduction to the concepts of writing modular code, which we will continue to explain in upcoming lessons.

Here is the program in its entirety. Step through it in the debugger a few times with different values to get a good feel for how it works.

```
print "First Down Calculator"
input "What down is it (1, 2, 3, or 4)?"; down
input "Yards to go for 1st down?"; yardsToGo
input "Yards advanced?"; yardsAdvanced
if yardsAdvanced >= yardsToGo then
    down = 1
    print "First down!"
else
```

```
        down = down + 1
        if down > 4 then
            down = 1
            print "Ball changes sides!"
        end if
        print "New down is: "; down
    end if
    end
```

Notice that each IF THEN has a matching END IF. This is an important requirement of the Liberty BASIC syntax.

Exercise - A Hi-Lo Game

Hi-Lo is a game where the computer has a secret number. The player tries to guess the number. If the player guesses too low the program responds with "Guess Higher" or if the player guesses too high the program responds with "Guess Lower". When the player guesses correctly the program responds with "You win. It took you *number* guesses!"

In order to have a secret number, the program can use the RND( ) function to create a random number. This special function is common in BASIC languages. Each time you use RND( ) it will return a different value between 0 and 1. So, to get a secret number between 1 and 100 we multiply the return from RND( ) by 100, add 1, and then get the integer value of that using the INT( ) function. I leave it to the student to look up the RND( ) and INT( ) functions in the Liberty BASIC help file.

Here is what the code for generating the secret number looks like. Use this in your program:

```
secretNumber = int(rnd(1)*100+1)
```

Here is an outline of what the program should do:

1) Print program title and give some instructions
2) Pick a secret number between 1 and 100
3) Ask for the user to guess number
4) Tally the guess
5) If the guess is right go to step (9)
6) If the guess is too low tell the user to guess higher
7) If the guess is too high tell the user to guess lower
8) Go back to step (3)
9) Beep and tell the user how many guess it took to win
10) Ask the user whether to play again
11) If the user answers yes then clear the guess tally and goto step (1)
12) Give the user instructions on how to close the game window
13) End the program

Try to write the program using nested IF THEN blocks.

Quiz - Answers further down the page

1) A _____ is used like an address.

2) The _____ command is used to direct program execution to a branch label.

3) Decisions are made in programs using the _____ command.

4) The symbols <, >, =, <>, <=, >= are known as _____.

5) Strings are compared _____ instead of alphabetically.

6) To make an IF THEN block, we need to wrap up with _____.

7) When an IF THEN block is inside another IF THEN block, this is known as a _____.

8) Each displayable alphanumeric symbol has an _____ value.

9) Program code that repeats is called a _____.

10) A loop that doesn't end is called an _____ loop.

Answers

1) branch label

2) GOTO

3) IF THEN

4) comparison operators

5) alphanumerically

6) END IF

7) nested block

8) ASCII

9) loop

9) infinite

Chapter Four

Getting Loopy with Iterators!

In order to do anything really interesting, computers need to do the same things over and over. The Hi-Lo game is a good example. If you only got to guess once for a number between 1 and 100, you might lose interest in guessing. If a word processor only let you type in one word, what good would it be? If your web browser could only show one web site it wouldn't be very useful. Even if you look at a single web page, if the web browser can not load each image on the page (this is done by looping), it would be ugly or unusable. Looping is important!

One reason to loop in a computer program is to repeat some action until a certain condition is met. For example in the Hi-Lo game we loop until the game is won. Another reason to loop is when we want to do something a very specific number of times. Here is an example from chapter three:

```
  print "L";
[oneMoreTime]
  print "OO";
  counter = counter + 1
  if counter < 10 then goto [oneMoreTime]
  print "PY!"
  end
```

A fancy word for a looping command is *iterator.*

Looping with WHILE/WEND

In Lesson Three we showed how to create loops using branch labels and the GOTO command. This is a fine way to create loops (they work), but most programming languages come with built-in iterators designed to make some kinds of looping easier and cleaner. One of these iterators is called WHILE/WEND. Here is what our program above would look like if we rewrote it to use WHILE/WEND:

```
  print "L";
  while counter < 10
```

51

```
  print "OO";
  counter = counter + 1
wend
print "PY!"
end
```

Try this program in the debugger to see how it works. The
WHILE/WEND iterator will loop as long as the comparison in the WHILE
command computes to true. So in our above example, as long as counter is
less than 10, the WHILE/WEND loop will repeat the code between
WHILE and WEND.

When using an iterator there is no need for a branch label. This can be
very nice because not all loops can have a more meaningful branch label
than [oneMoreTime]. If your program has more than a few loops, it can be
hard to create a different name for each branch label. WHILE/WEND can
save you from creating programs with branch labels named
[againAndAgain], [oneMoreTime], [rinseAndRepeat], [playItAgainSam],
etc. ;-)

Another interesting feature of a WHILE/WEND loop is that the code
inside the loop will never execute if the comparison is false to begin with.
Execution will just skip right over the loop. Let's add a line of code to the
beginning of the program to show how this works:

```
counter = 10
print "L";
while counter < 10
  print "OO";
  counter = counter + 1
wend
print "PY!"
end
```

What do you think will be the printed output of this program? If you
guessed LPY! then you guessed right! The code that prints the letters OO
just gets skipped right over. Here is what the code would look like if you
wrote it using branch labels and GOTOs.

```
counter = 10
print "L";
if counter >= 10 then [skipOver]
[oneMoreTime]
  print "OO";
```

```
  counter = counter + 1
  if counter < 10 then [oneMoreTime]
[skipOver]
  print "PY!"
  end
```

Looping with FOR/NEXT

These examples show how to loop until a condition is met, but they also demonstrate how to loop until a certain count is reached. BASIC has a special iterator for looping and counting at the same time. This is called FOR/NEXT.

Let's look at how our example above looks rewritten to use FOR/NEXT:

```
  print "L";
  for counter = 1 to 10
    print "OO";
  next counter
  print "PY!"
  end
```

This is the shortest and simplest version of the program so far. This is because the counting part is done for us. There is no `counter = counter + 1` line needed.

Here is how it works:

  - The FOR command sets counter to 1 and sets a limit of 10.
  - The PRINT command is executed.
  - The NEXT command increases counter by 1.
  - If counter hasn't reached the limit of 10, we loop back and repeat .

Try the example in the debugger. If is still isn't clear that the program is counting, maybe this example will make it clearer.

```
  for counter = 1 to 10
    print "value is "; counter
  next counter
  end
```

Realize that we can choose any valid variable name. This works just as well:

53

```
for chickens = 1 to 10
  print "value is "; chickens
next chickens
end
```

Also, we don't have to start at one and end at ten.

```
for counter = 5 to 8
  print "value is "; counter
next counter
end
```

A special STEP option allows us to specify how much to add (instead of always counting by 1), so we don't have to count by one.

```
for counter = 1 to 9 step 2
  print "value is "; counter
next counter
end
```

And STEP can even be used to count backwards, like this:

```
for counter = 10 to 1 step -1
  print "value is "; counter
next counter
end
```

More blocks - Just like the code between an IF THEN and END IF is called a block, so also the code inside a WHILE/WEND is called a *WHILE/WEND block* and code inside a FOR/NEXT loop is called a *FOR/NEXT block*.

Fun with Strings

Let's try some fun things with strings and iterators. By using WHILE/WEND and the WORD$( ) function that we covered earlier, we can make a short program that counts the words in a sentence:

```
input "Please type a sentence?"; sentence$
while reachedEnd = 0
  position = position + 1
  if word$(sentence$, position) <> "" then
    wordCount = wordCount + 1
```

```
      else
         reachedEnd = 1
      end if
   wend
   print "You typed "; wordCount; " words."
   end
```

Can you guess how this works? The WORD$( ) function allows you to
extract the the word from a string at the position you specify. If there is no
word at that position, it will return an empty string. So we know once we
get an empty string that we have counted all the words, and we set
reachedEnd to 1. This causes the WHILE/WEND loop to end.

Here's another fun one. Let's write a program that reverses a string. The
first character will be at the end of the new reversed string, and the last
character will be at the beginning. To do this, we need to introduce a
couple of new functions.

First we'll look at the LEN( ) function. This function tells us how many
characters are in a string, so for example:

```
   howLong$ = "Liberty BASIC"
   print len(howLong$); " characters long."
   end
```

Secondly there is the MID$( ) function. This function lets you cut pieces
out of a string to make a smaller string. Here is an example of using the
MID$( ) function to take single character out of the middle of a string.

```
   phrase$ = "What looks like a donut?"
   print phrase$
   snack$ = mid$(phrase$, 20, 1)
   print snack$
   end
```

The MID$( ) function in this example takes 1 character out of the string in
phrase$ starting at the 20th character.

Now we are ready to write a program to reverse a string:

```
reverseMe$ = "this is forwards -- sdrawkcab si siht"
print reverseMe$
for pointer = 1 to len(reverseMe$)
  reversed$ = mid$(reverseMe$, pointer, 1) + reversed$
next pointer
print reversed$
end
```

Step through this in the debugger. See how the new string reversed$ is built a character at a time? Each character is added to the *front* of the new string. Can you think of a way to do this by adding characters to the end? Here is one way:

```
reverseMe$ = "guess my name! -- nikstlitselpmuR"
print reverseMe$
for pointer = len(reverseMe$) to 1 step -1
  reversed$ = reversed$ + mid$(reverseMe$, pointer, 1)
next pointer
print reversed$
end
```

We do it by counting backwards using STEP -1!

Good Practices – Nested Blocks

Take a look at the following code. The FOR has a matching NEXT, and the IF THEN has a matching END IF, but is wrong. Can you spot what is wrong with it?

```
stuff$ = "count the spaces in this string"
print stuff$
for pointer = 1 to len(stuff$)
  char$ = mid$(stuff$, pointer, 1)
  if char$ = " " then
    counter = counter + 1
    next pointer
  end if
print counter
end
```

The FOR/NEXT and IF THEN/END IF blocks overlap, and they should not.

They are structured like this (WRONG):

```
for ----------
             |
   if then-- |
          |  |
     next---+--
          |
   end if---
```

They should look like this:

```
for-----------
             |
   if then-- |
          |  |
   end if--- |
             |
next----------
```

Here is the corrected program:

```
stuff$ = "count the spaces in this string"
print stuff$
for pointer = 1 to len(stuff$)
  char$ = mid$(stuff$, pointer, 1)
  if char$ = " " then
    counter = counter + 1
  end if
next pointer
print counter
end
```

Blocks should always be properly nested.

Here is another example with a problem:

```
stuff$ = "find the Z in this string"
print stuff$
for pointer = 1 to len(stuff$)
  char$ = mid$(stuff$, pointer, 1)
  if char$ = "Z" then goto [foundIt]
next pointer
[foundIt]
  print "Z at location "; pointer
  end
```

57

If you run the program, it seems to work just fine. However, using GOTO to break out of a FOR/NEXT loop is a good way to confuse Liberty BASIC. Instead, always use the EXIT FOR command, which tells Liberty BASIC to terminate the FOR/NEXT loop and jump to the next line after the NEXT command. Here is a fixed version:

```
stuff$ = "find the Z in this string"
print stuff$
for pointer = 1 to len(stuff$)
  char$ = mid$(stuff$, pointer, 1)
  if char$ = "Z" then exit for
next pointer
print "Z at location "; pointer
end
```

Similarly, using GOTO to jump into a loop is a bad idea. In many programming languages it isn't even possible.

```
'not a good idea
goto [jumpIn]

for x = 1 to 10
  [jumpIn]
  print x
next x
```

Many times programmers are told that using GOTO is a bad practice and that it leads to unmaintainable code. I say don't overuse GOTO, but use the right tool for the job. GOTO can do things that other commands cannot. For example if we make a loop using GOTO instead of FOR and NEXT we can jump out of the loop to any place in the program either before or after the loop.

```
'Try this with a FOR/NEXT loop
search$ = "here is the letter z"

[searchForZLoop]
  position = position + 1
  if mid$(search$, position, 1) = "z" then [foundIt]
  if position = len(search$) then [notFound]
  goto [searchForZLoop]

[notFound]
  print "z not found"
  end

[foundIt]
  print "z found at "; position
  end
```

Exercise One - Words from a sentence

Without using the WORD$( ) function, write a program which will ask for a sentence from the user and then print out the words in the sentence as shown below. Use a FOR/NEXT loop.

Enter a sentence? The quick brown fox jumped over the lazy dog.
The
quick
brown
fox
jumped
over
the
lazy
dog

Exercise Two - Average some numbers

Using a WHILE/WEND loop, write a program which asks the user for a series of numbers. The program will count each number the user enters. When the user types end, produce the average for the numbers the user entered. To produce the average, add all the numbers together that the user entered, and divide by the count. For example:

Enter some numbers to average.
? 32
? 10
? 3
? end
You entered 3 numbers.
The average is 15

Hint: Use a string variable to get the user's entries. If the user enters the word end, stop asking for more entries and compute the average. If the user doesn't enter the word end, convert their entry into a numeric value using the VAL( ) function.

Quiz - Answers on the next page

1) A special programming language feature for looping is called an
_____.

2) Iterators do not need branch _____.

3) The _____ iterator counts each time it loops.

4) The _____ iterator loops according to a true or false
result.

5) Never use _____ to break out of a FOR/NEXT loop.

6) To count backwards in a FOR/NEXT loop, use
_____.

7) Get a portion of a string using the _____ function.

8) Code blocks should never _____.

9) To break out of a FOR/NEXT loop, use _____.

10) To get the length of a string, use the _____ function.

11) nikstlitselpmuR is _____ spelled backwards. ;-)

Answers

1) iterator

2) labels

3) FOR/NEXT

4) WHILE/WEND

5) GOTO

6) STEP

7) MID$( )

8) overlap

9) EXIT FOR

10) LEN( )

11) Rumplestiltskin

Chapter Five

Software as System - Refactoring and Reuse

When programs begin to grow beyond a page or so of code they can begin to become hard to work with. Without some care and good practices, the *meaning* of a computer program can become lost. This isn't about the meaning according to the computer. The computer will never know (or care) what the program means, but if the computer can execute the code that will be enough for the computer. What does the program mean when a person reads the code? That's what I meant!

When people build something complicated, they build it out of parts. We don't say about a car, "This piece of metal is attached to this other piece of metal with another piece of metal," do we? No, of course not! We say, "This water pump is bolted onto the engine block!" Each part does something special and each part has an equally special name. We will learn to build software this way, as a system made out of parts named for the special part they play.

Modularity

In an earlier lesson we covered the idea of the *intention revealing* variable name. This is the careful choice of a variable name to communicate to the programmer what the purpose of the variable is. This idea is central to writing good software, and not just for variables.

The intention revealing idea also makes sense for branch labels. When you have a `goto [announceWin]` in your Hi-Lo game program, this communicates what is going to happen a lot better than `goto [routineA]`. The code at `[youWin]` is a part (a *module* if you like) of the program, and it should do what it's name implies. In this way, a branch label can be intention revealing. Let's take a look at how to use this idea using our Hi-Lo program from the chapter three exercise:

```
[start]
  guessMe = int(rnd(1)*100 + 1)
  print "HI-LO"
  print
  print "I have decided on a number between one"
  print "and a hundred, and I want you to guess"
  print "what it is.  I will tell you to guess"
  print "higher or lower, and we'll count up"
  print "the number of guesses you use."
  print
[ask]
  input "OK.  What is your guess?"; guess
  count = count + 1
  if guess = guessMe then
    print "You win!  It took"; count; "guesses."
    guess = 0
    count = 0
    input "Play again (y/n)"; play$
    if play$ = "y" then [start]
    print "Press ALT+F4 to close this window."
    end
  else
    if guess < guessMe then
      print "Guess higher."
    else
      print "Guess lower."
    end if
  end if
  goto [ask]
  end
```

This is a simple program. We have the [start] and [ask] branch
labels giving us some idea what happens at those points. After that we are
on our own. One way we can make it more clear is to break some of the
code out of the program into a named module called a *subroutine*. Let's
see what this would look like:

```
[start]
  guessMe = int(rnd(1)*100 + 1)
  print "HI-LO"
  print
  print "I have decided on a number between one"
  print "and a hundred, and I want you to guess"
  print "what it is.  I will tell you to guess"
  print "higher or lower, and we'll count up"
  print "the number of guesses you use."
  print
```

```
[ask]
  input "OK.  What is your guess?"; guess
  count = count + 1
  if guess = guessMe then
    gosub [announceWin]
    input "Play again (y/n)"; play$
    if play$ = "y" then [start]
    print "Press ALT+F4 to close this window."
    end
  else
    if guess < guessMe then
      print "Guess higher."
    else
      print "Guess lower."
    end if
  end if
  goto [ask]
[announceWin]
  print "You win!  It took"; count; "guesses."
  guess = 0
  count = 0
  return
  end
```

Look at the end of the program. We broke some code out and gave it a branch label *[announceWin]*, which names the subroutine (the whole subroutine is in bold, italic type). The end of the subroutine is marked by the RETURN command. Now, look above to where the code was. We replaced the code with *gosub [announceWin]*. Reorganizing code in this way, where it still does the same thing but has a different structure is called *refactoring*.

The GOSUB command is a special kind of GOTO. After the GOSUB command causes a branch to a subroutine, code executes normally until a RETURN command is encountered. When this happens, Liberty BASIC remembers the GOSUB that called the subroutine and goes back to the point *right after* that GOSUB and *returns* to continue execution there. Think of it as a bookmark. You want to peek at some other place in a book, so you place a bookmark (or your thumb) so you find your place. When you are done looking around, you *return* to the bookmark and continue reading. This is how GOSUB and RETURN work. Step through the program in the debugger to see exactly how it works.

This technique gives us more intention revealing markers to look at. We can take it even further. For example:

65

```
[start]
  guessMe = int(rnd(1)*100 + 1)
  print "HI-LO"
  print
  print "I have decided on a number between one"
  print "and a hundred, and I want you to guess"
  print "what it is.  I will tell you to guess"
  print "higher or lower, and we'll count up"
  print "the number of guesses you use."
  print
[ask]
  input "OK.  What is your guess?"; guess
  count = count + 1
  if guess = guessMe then
    gosub [announceWin]
    input "Play again (y/n)"; play$
    if play$ = "y" then [start]
    print "Press ALT+F4 to close this window."
    end
  else
    gosub [giveHint]
  end if
  goto [ask]
[announceWin]
  print "You win!  It took"; count; "guesses."
  guess = 0
  count = 0
  return
[giveHint]
  if guess < guessMe then
    print "Guess higher."
  else
    print "Guess lower."
  end if
  return
  end
```

See how we refactor the program by taking the code that says "Guess higher." or "Guess lower." and make a subroutine out of it (in bold italics)?

Reuse

One really important idea behind subroutines is called *reuse* (re-use), which is when you have code written once that is used in more than one place. This can be accomplished with GOSUB/RETURN. Look at this survey program for an example of code that is just ripe for a little reuse:

```
print "Survey - What are computers good for?"
print
input "Are they good for eating (Y/N)?"; answer$
while answerAccepted = 0
  if answer$ = "Y" then
    yesCount = yesCount + 1
    answerAccepted = 1
  else
    if answer$ = "N" then
      answerAccepted = 1
    else
      input "Bad input. Answer Y or N?"; answer$
    end if
  end if
wend
totalAnswers = totalAnswers + 1
print
input "Are they good for wasting time (Y/N)?"; answer$
answerAccepted = 0
while answerAccepted = 0
  if answer$ = "Y" then
    yesCount = yesCount + 1
    answerAccepted = 1
  else
    if answer$ = "N" then
      answerAccepted = 1
    else
      input "Bad input. Answer Y or N?"; answer$
    end if
  end if
wend
totalAnswers = totalAnswers + 1
print
input "Are they good for a laugh (Y/N)?"; answer$
answerAccepted = 0
while answerAccepted = 0
  if answer$ = "Y" then
    yesCount = yesCount + 1
    answerAccepted = 1
  else
    if answer$ = "N" then
      answerAccepted = 1
    else
      input "Bad input. Answer Y or N?"; answer$
    end if
  end if
wend
totalAnswers = totalAnswers + 1
```

```
print "Results:"
print yesCount; " of "; totalAnswers; " Y answers"
end
```

Our program asks three questions, but most of the code is just about making sure the user enters correctly a letter Y or N for the answer. There is a *lot* of duplicated code. This makes it hard to read, and it's wasteful. Now let's look at how this program looks after we refactor it to make the repetitive code into just one subroutine:

```
print "Survey - What are computers good for?"
print
input "Are they grail shaped (Y/N)?"; answer$
gosub [checkForCorrectAnswer]
print
input "Are they good babysitters (Y/N)?"; answer$
gosub [checkForCorrectAnswer]
print
input "Do they prevent tooth decay (Y/N)?"; answer$
gosub [checkForCorrectAnswer]
print "Results:"
print yesCount; " of "; totalAnswers; " Y answers"
end
[checkForCorrectAnswer]
  answerAccepted = 0
  while answerAccepted = 0
    if answer$ = "Y" then
      yesCount = yesCount + 1
      print yesCount
      answerAccepted = 1
    else
      if answer$ = "N" then
        answerAccepted = 1
      else
        input "Bad input. Answer Y or N?"; answer$
      end if
    end if
  wend
  totalAnswers = totalAnswers + 1
  return
  end
```

This version of the program is much smaller because after each survey question we use the GOSUB command to call a subroutine that checks the user's answer to make sure it is Y or N. It is as though the code in the subroutine exists in every place where the GOSUB [checkForCorrectAnswer] is used (three places in this example), but the logic is coded in only one *reusable* module.

Idea Break! - Many Happy Returns

One mistake that beginners often make with GOSUB is that they forget to use RETURN with it. A subroutine should always finish its work with RETURN. Look at this example:

```
'How not to use GOSUB
capitalizeThis$ = "the quick brown fox"
GOSUB [capitalize]

[printIt]
  print capitalized$
  end

[capitalize]
  capitalized$ = upper$(capitalizeThis$)
  goto [printIt]
```

Instead of GOTO, that last line of code should be a RETURN statement. Be careful not to use GOSUB like GOTO. Each time GOSUB is executed it will use a little more memory. Then if no RETURN statements are executed that memory will never get released and the program will consume more and more memory.

CALL and SUB

Sometimes it can be hard to write reusable code with GOSUB/RETURN. The biggest problem is that each section of code in your program that wants to use a subroutine may have different variable names for the things you want your subroutine to work on. This makes for a little extra work. Have a look at this example. *We use the UPPER$( ) function which converts all the letters in a string to uppercase.*

```
input "Customer name?"; customerName$

input "Address?"; address$
input "City?"; city$
print "You entered:"
```

```
  capitalizeThis$ = customerName$
  gosub [printCapitalized]
  capitalizeThis$ = address$
  gosub [printCapitalized]
  capitalizeThis$ = city$
  gosub [printCapitalized]
  end
[printCapitalized]
  lastChar$ = ""
  result$ = ""
  for x = 1 to len(capitalizeThis$)
    char$ = mid$(capitalizeThis$, x, 1)
    if lastChar$ = "" then
      char$ = upper$(char$)
    else
      if lastChar$ = " " then
        char$ = upper$(char$)
      end if
    end if
    result$ = result$ + char$
    lastChar$ = char$
  next x
  print result$
  return
```

This example asks for a customer name, an address, and a city (we could go further of course) and then prints these three things out with the first letter of each word capitalized. It uses a subroutine `[printCapitalized]` to display each thing capitalized. This is a nice example of reuse, right? Yes, and no. We can do better:

```
input "Customer name?"; customerName$

input "Address?"; address$
input "City?"; city$
print "You entered:"
call printCapitalized customerName$
call printCapitalized address$
call printCapitalized city$
end

sub printCapitalized capitalizeThis$
  for x = 1 to len(capitalizeThis$)
    char$ = mid$(capitalizeThis$, x, 1)
    if lastChar$ = "" then
      char$ = upper$(char$)
    else
      if lastChar$ = " " then
```

```
      char$ = upper$(char$)
    end if
  end if
  result$ = result$ + char$
  lastChar$ = char$
 next x
 print result$
end sub
```

We replace the branch label and RETURN command from the first example with SUB and END SUB commands. We can execute this subroutine with a CALL command. This creates another kind of subroutine which works similarly to the GOSUB/RETURN type we looked at earlier, but it has a very special feature. This kind of subroutine has its own variables, which cannot be seen by program code outside of the subroutine. It also works the other way. The code inside the subroutine cannot see variables outside. This is a common feature of many programming languages, called *scope*. If a variable is visible in one place, this is called *local scope* and if a variable is visible everywhere this is called *global scope*.

In order for our example program above to insert the string values from customerName$, address$, and city$ into the printCapitalized subroutine, the subroutine must first declare that it requires a value from the outside. Here is the SUB command from the program. It declares a subroutine named printCapitalized which expects a string value which it will assign to the variable named capitalizeThis$.

```
sub printCapitalized capitalizeThis$
```

Then when we want to use the subroutine, we provide a string value to the subroutine using the CALL command, like so:

```
call printCapitalized customerName$
```

When this CALL command is executed and as the subroutine begins to do its work, the value of customerName$ gets assigned to capitalizeThis$.

Then, once that assignment happens, the subroutine executes until it reaches the END SUB. This is just like a RETURN command. The program goes back to executing the next thing right after the CALL. Try stepping through the example in the debugger.

71

You aren't limited to just one parameterized value when you define a subroutine. You can have a dozen or so if you really need them. Here is an example with three parameters (notice the commas between the parameters):

```
call printFromTo "Chop me up!", 6, 7
end

sub printFromTo source$, beginPosition, endPosition
  for x = beginPosition to endPosition
    print mid$(source$, x, 1);
  next x
end sub
```

One really useful feature of scoping is that you can use the same variable names in different subroutines and they will not conflict. A variable named count in the program's main code could hold the number of survey questions answered, and another variable named count in another subroutine might be used to count the number of times the answer was Y. Here is a really short program that shows how two variables with the same name in two different places each have their own values independent of each other:

```
for count = 1 to 5
  print "Counting to "; count
  countThese$ = word$("little pigs let me in", count)
  call countLetters countThese$
next count
end

sub countLetters countThese$
  count = len(countThese$)
  print count; " letters in "; countThese$
end sub
```

The variable count used by the FOR/NEXT loop has the same name as the variable count inside the countLetters subroutine, but they are actually different variables with their own unique values. If you tried to do this with GOSUB/RETURN the program wouldn't work correctly. The following does not work correctly unless you resolve the variable name conflict by renaming the count variable in the subroutine to some other name:

```
for count = 1 to 5
  print "Counting to "; count
  countThese$ = word$("little pigs let me in", count)
  gosub [countLetters]
next count
end

[countLetters]
  count = len(countThese$)
  print count; " letters in "; countThese$
  return
```

You only need to run this example to see the value in being able to use the same variable name in different places. The FOR/NEXT loop should seem to loop 5 times, counting to 5, but it doesn't. It's such a simple thing, and it doesn't work! The reason isn't revealed until you examine the subroutine. The bigger your program becomes, the more valuable local scoping becomes. The more code you write, the more you will want to reuse code between programs. This is a much easier matter if you don't have to worry about conflicting variable names. With local scoping, just copy and paste the subroutine between programs, and you're good.

User Functions

Sometimes we want to be able to get a value back from a subroutine. With a GOSUB/RETURN style subroutine this is not a problem because all the variables in the subroutine are visible to the calling code. Since subroutines defined using SUB have no way to return a value, sometimes this can be a good enough reason to choose GOSUB/RETURN over CALL and SUB. We do have a partial solution to this problem. Have a look at this version of the capitalization example refactored to use a user function.

```
input "Customer name?"; customerName$
input "Address?"; address$
input "City?"; city$
print "You entered:"
print capitalize$(customerName$)
print capitalize$(address$)
print capitalize$(city$)
end

function capitalize$(capitalizeThis$)
  for x = 1 to len(capitalizeThis$)
    char$ = mid$(capitalizeThis$, x, 1)
```

```
      if lastChar$ = "" then
        char$ = upper$(char$)
      else
        if lastChar$ = " " then
          char$ = upper$(char$)
        end if
      end if
      result$ = result$ + char$
      lastChar$ = char$
    next x
    capitalize$ = result$
end function
```

This is very similar to the prior example that uses SUB/END SUB but instead it uses FUNCTION/END FUNCTION. A user function is also a kind of subroutine, but it returns value. You use it just like you use Liberty BASIC's built-in functions like STR$( ), WORD$( ), etc. What can you do with the returned value?

- print it out
- assign it to a variable
- use it as part of a larger expression

Look at the line in the example above before the `end function` command:

```
    capitalize$ = result$
```

This line tells the function to return the value in `result$` when the function ends. We could have just used the `capitalize$` variable name instead of `result$`, and then there would be no need to reassign the value of `result$` to `capitalize$`.

Here is what that user function would look like:

```
function capitalize$(capitalizeThis$)
  for x = 1 to len(capitalizeThis$)
    char$ = mid$(capitalizeThis$, x, 1)
    if lastChar$ = "" then
      char$ = upper$(char$)
    else
      if lastChar$ = " " then
        char$ = upper$(char$)
      end if
    end if
    capitalize$ = capitalize$ + char$
    lastChar$ = char$
  next x
```

```
end function
```

Notice the $ in the name of the function. This specifies that the function returns a string. If we want to return a numeric value the function name cannot end in a $. Here is a simple little example of a function that returns a numeric value:

```
print "Square calculator"
input "Enter a number?"; number
print square(number)
end
```

```
function square(aValue)
  square = aValue * aValue
end function
```

See how we set the `square` variable to be the value we want to return from the user function? It is the same as the name of the function.

Exercise One - String Commander

Write a program called String Commander that asks the user for a string. Then it asks the user to type a command which performs some action on that string. It displays:

- the name of the command
- the string before the command executes
- the string now (after the command)

The program also has a simple help facility. Here is what the program should look like when it runs:

```
String Commander
Please type a string? Rubber baby buggy bumpers

Please type a command (Enter for help)? User presses Enter

Help, List of commands:
UPPER - Convert the string to uppercase
VOWELS - Strip out all non-vowels
NOSPACES - Strip out all spaces
UNDO - Revert to the original string the user typed in
QUIT - End the program
```

```
Please type a command (Enter for help)? NOSPACES

Operation: NOSPACES
String was: Rubber baby buggy bumpers
String now: Rubberbabybuggybumpers

Please type a command (Enter for help)? VOWELS

Operation: VOWELS
String was: Rubberbabybuggybumpers
String now: uerauue

Please type a command (Enter for help)? NOSPACES

Operation: UPPER
String was: uerauue
String now: UERAUUE

Please type a command (Enter for help)? UNDO

Operation: UNDO
String was: uerauue
String now: Rubber baby buggy bumpers

Please type a command (Enter for help)? QUIT

Program ended.
```

Write this program using GOSUB and RETURN. There should be a subroutine to execute each command that modifies the string, and a subroutine that does the display after each command.

Exercise Two - String Commander

Take the String Commander and modify it to use CALL and SUB for the display subroutine, and user functions (FUNCTION/END FUNCTION) to execute the commands that modify the string.

Quiz - Answers on the next page

1) Another name for a named program module is a
_____.

2) Reorganizing a program's code without changing the way it works is
called _____.

3) A subroutine called using GOSUB ends with the _____
command.

4) To return a value from a user function, assign the _____
named after the user function.

5) _____ is writing code once and using it in more than one
place.

6) SUB/END SUB are used to begin and end a kind of
_____.

7) The command used to call a SUB/END SUB subroutine is
_____.

8) Variables in a SUB/END SUB subroutine have _____
scope.

9) FUNCTION/END FUNCTION are used to begin and end a
_____ function.

Answers

1) subroutine

2) refactoring

3) RETURN

4) variable

5) reuse

6) subroutine

7) CALL

8) local

9) user

Chapter 6

Using Arrays to Manage Lists of Things

Computers are more often than not used to keep track of lists of things. These could be lists of customers, lists of stock #'s, or lists of fonts. A list of things doesn't even have to look like a list. For an example of this, take a look at your favorite video games. If you've ever played PacMan or Quake, the monsters are managed in one kind of list or another (but you never see the list).

In most programming languages, these lists are called *arrays*.

To see why we need arrays, let's look at what programming for lists looks like without arrays. Suppose we want to keep track of a list of up to 10 computers. Using only the techniques we've covered so far it would look like this

```
'NOARRAY.BAS
'Computer audit list handling - without an array
print "CAP Pro - Computer Auditing Program"

[askForId]  'ask for an ID
  input "Enter a computer ID?"; entry$
  if entry$ = "" then print "No entry." : goto [quit]
  if id1$ = "" then id1$ = entry$ : goto [added]
  if id2$ = "" then id2$ = entry$ : goto [added]
  if id3$ = "" then id3$ = entry$ : goto [added]
  if id4$ = "" then id4$ = entry$ : goto [added]
  if id5$ = "" then id5$ = entry$ : goto [added]
  if id6$ = "" then id6$ = entry$ : goto [added]
  if id7$ = "" then id7$ = entry$ : goto [added]
  if id8$ = "" then id8$ = entry$ : goto [added]
  if id9$ = "" then id9$ = entry$ : goto [added]
  if id10$ = "" then id10$ = entry$ : goto [added]
  'There weren't any available slots, inform user
  print "All ten slots are already used!"
  print "You don't need that many computers, do you?"
  goto [quit]

[added]    'Notify the ID add was successful
  print entry$; " has been added to the list."
```

79

```
  goto [askForId]

[quit]
  end
```

In this example when we enter an ID, the computer will look at up to ten variables in turn, id1$ through id10$. If it finds a variable that is an empty string, it will set the value of that variable to be equal to id$. Then it will GOTO [added] and display a notice that the ID has been added. If this were part of a larger program, we would execute this code whenever we wanted to add an ID, and the ID would be inserted into the next available slot.

This technique is manageable only for very small lists. If you're like me, you must have computers coming out of your ears. Ten slots isn't nearly enough. Imagine how many lines of code we would need to track hundreds or thousands of items in this way! Arrays provide a special way to make a little bit of code refer to any one variable out of a list of thousands (or millions).

Here is our computer list example rewritten using a BASIC array. If it seems unclear to you, try running the debugger on it.

```
  'ARRAY.BAS
  'Computer audit list handling - with an array
  dim id$(10)  'set up our array to contain 10 strings
  print "CAP Pro - Computer Auditing Program"

[askForId]  'ask for an ID
  input "Enter an ID?"; entry$
  if entry$ = "" then
    print "No ID entered."
    goto [quit]
  end if

  index = 0  'reset to beginning
[insert]
  'if index points to an empty slot in array, fill it
  if id$(index) = "" then
    id$(index) = entry$
    goto [idAdded]
  end if
  index = index + 1 'add 1 to index
  if index < 10 then [insert] 'repeat with next slot
```

```
'There weren't any available slots, inform user
print "All slots already used."
print "You're lucky this program uses an array! ;-)"
goto [quit]

[idAdded]   'Notify the add was successful
  print entry$; " has been added to the list."
  goto [askForId]

[quit]
  end
```

Notice the dim id$(10) statement at the start of this example. This tells BASIC to create an array called id$ with room for 10 items. Because the name of the array ends with a $ character, this is an array of strings (remember that a string variable name ends with a $). So at first, the array is full of empty strings "". Arrays can hold numbers too. An array that holds numbers has a name with no $ character. The first item in an array is referred to by the value 0, and so an array of 10 items starts with item 0 and ends with item 9.

The real work is done in this part of the code:

```
  index = 0   'reset to beginning
[insert]
  'if index points to an empty slot in array, fill it
  if id$(index) = "" then
    id$(index) = entry$
    goto [idAdded]
  end if
  index = index + 1 'add 1 to index
  if index < 10 then [insert] 'repeat with next slot
```

Here we are using a simple loop to control a search for an empty slot in our array id$( ). Take a look at this part of the program:

```
  if id$(index) = "" then
    id$(index) = entry$
    goto [idAdded]
  end if
```

The if id$(index) = "" then part of the code uses the value of index to point to a particular string in the array. Just think of the array as

81

having a bunch of variables and each has an address, like houses on a street (except that houses don't usually have a number 0). When index = 0, we are looking at the first item in the array. When the code loops back and index is 1, it will be looking at the second item in the array, and so on.

The `id$(index) = entry$` part of the code assigns the value of entry$ to the array position selected by index. This isn't really different from assigning a value to any other variable.

Notice that we get the value of an item in an array by its position using a numeric value. We also choose a position and perform assignment by using a numeric value. In programming, a list of things managed by numeric position is sometimes called an *indexed collection*.

Our ARRAY.BAS example is a little more complicated than NOARRAY.BAS, but it has the advantage of size. If we discover after writing this program that we need to manage 1000 items, we only need to change our code a little bit. Here is what the modified program looks like (changes in bold italics):

```
'ARRAY.BAS
'Computer audit list handling - with an array
dim id$(1000) 'set up an array to contain 1000 strings
print "CAP Pro - Computer Auditing Program"

[askForId]  'ask for an ID
  input "Enter an ID?"; entry$
  if entry$ = "" then
    print "No ID entered."
    goto [quit]
  end if

  index = 0   'reset to beginning
[insert]
  'if index points to an empty slot in array, fill it
  if id$(index) = "" then
    id$(index) = entry$
    goto [idAdded]
  end if
  index = index + 1 'add 1 to index
  if index < 1000 then [insert] 'repeat with next slot

  'There weren't any available slots, inform user
  print "All slots already used."
  print "You're lucky this program uses an array! ;-)"
```

```
    goto [quit]

[idAdded]  'Notify the add was successful
  print entry$; " has been added to the list."
  goto [askForId]

[quit]
  end
```

See how we only needed to modify the lines that are related to the size of our array? We only need to modify the DIM command, and the line that checks the index to see if it has reached the size limit of the array. If we tried to extend our first example NOARRAY.BAS to manage 1000 names, it would become monstrously large! The resulting program would have more than one line of code for each slot we needed to manage. Can you say "thousands of lines of code"? I think you can!

When we have a programming technique that works well for small sets of data, but that doesn't work well when things get large, we say that it doesn't *scale*. Our NOARRAY.BAS example uses a technique that doesn't scale. We solve this scaling problem in the ARRAY.BAS example using arrays and loops.

So, arrays are our friends!

Index Out of Bounds

Try running the following mini program.

```
'done wrong
dim names$(10)
print names$(15)
```

You will get an error message saying 'system primitive failed'. This sounds ominous, but in this case it just means that you tried to print the contents of an array item that doesn't exist. This is often called an *out of bounds* error. If you dimension the array to make it large enough, it will work.

```
'done right
dim names$(20)
print names$(15)
```

83

A similar error will occur if you try to set the item of an array using an index that is too large.

```
'done wrong again
dim names$(10)
names$(15) = "John Doe"
```

Idea Break! - Bounds Checking

It's good to make sure a program doesn't stop running with an error when the index goes out of bounds. So we can use IF/THEN to check the value of the index to be sure. Here is an example:

```
'set the size of our array
size = 3
dim color$(size)
color$(1) = "red"
color$(2) = "green"
color$(3) = "blue"

[getInput]
input "Pick a color (1=red,2=green,3=blue)"; index
'now we'll do the bounds checking
if index > 0 and index < size then
  print "you picked "; color$(index)
else
  print "Ooops.  Bad value."
  goto [getInput]
end if
```

Playing the numbers

Numeric arrays work very much like their relative the string array (featured above in ARRAYS.BAS). To demonstrate how numeric arrays work, examine this program that asks for some numbers, adds them up, and calculates the average value.

```
'AVERAGE.BAS
'Accept some numbers, then total and average them
dim numbers(20)
```

84

```
print "AVERAGE.BAS"
print

'loop up to 20 times, getting numbers
print "Enter up to 20 non-zero values."
print "A zero or blank entry ends the series."

[entryLoop] 'loop until a zero entry or until index = 20

'get the user's entry
print "Entry "; index + 1;
input entry$
if entry$ = "" then [endSeries]
entry = val(entry$)

numbers(index) = entry   'set the array item to be entry
index = index + 1        'add one to index
if index < 20 then [entryLoop]  'get another entry

[endSeries]  'entries are finished
'Set entryCount to index
entryCount = index
if entryCount = 0 then print "No Entries." : end
print "Entries completed."
print
print "Here are the "; entryCount; " entries:"
print "----------------------------"
for index = 0 to entryCount - 1
  print "Entry "; index + 1; " is "; numbers(index)
next index

'Now display the total and average value
for index = 0 to entryCount - 1
  total = total + numbers(index)
next index
print
print "The total is "; total
print "The average is "; total / entryCount

[quit]
end
```

Try stepping through this program with the debugger.

Arrays are globally scoped

One interesting and useful thing about arrays in Liberty BASIC is that they are globally scoped. This is in contrast to variables, which are locally scoped. This is important because you cannot pass an array as a parameter into a subroutine or user function, so having arrays be visible everywhere gets around this problem. The downside to global scoping of arrays is that we don't get the benefits that local scoping buys us.

Here's a short example of how global scoping of arrays makes them visible inside and outside of subroutines and user functions:

```
  dim myArray$(3)
  myArray$(0) = "I"
  myArray$(1) = "am"
  myArray$(2) = "globally"
  myArray$(3) = "scoped"
  call showMyArray
  end

sub showMyArray
  for x = 0 to 3
    print myArray$(x)
  next x
end sub
```

See how we are able to use the array named myArray$ inside of the subroutine showMyArray? We didn't have to do anything special at all. It just works.

Here is the averages program refactored to put most of its functionality inside of subroutines and a user function. Notice that the basic outline of the program can be read in the first dozen lines or so (in bold italics):

- get the entries
- display the entries
- and display the results

This technique of narrating the meaning of a program using intention revealing subroutine names as shown here is called *composed factoring*. You read it, and it says what it does.

```basic
'AVERAGE_REFACTORED.BAS
'Accept some numbers, then total and average them
dim numbers(20)
print "AVERAGE_REFACTORED.BAS"
print

'loop up to 20 times, getting numbers
print "Enter up to 20 non-zero values."
print "A zero or blank entry ends the series."

count = getEntries()
if count = 0 then print "No entries." : end
call displayEntries count
call displayResults count
goto [quit]

'Get numbers from the user.  Return the count
function getEntries()
  [entryLoop]
    'get the user's entry
    print "Entry "; index + 1;
    input entry$
    if entry$ = "" then [endSeries]
    entry = val(entry$)
    numbers(index) = entry  'assign the array item
    index = index + 1        'add one to index
    if index < 20 then [entryLoop]  'get another entry
  [endSeries]  'entries are finished
    getEntries = index
end function

'Display the list of numbers entered
sub displayEntries entryCount
  print "Entries completed."
  print
  print "Here are the "; entryCount; " entries:"
  print "---------------------------"
  for index = 0 to entryCount - 1
    print "Entry "; index + 1; " is "; numbers(index)
  next index
end sub

'Total up the entries.  Display total and average.
sub displayResults entryCount
  for index = 0 to entryCount - 1
    total = total + numbers(index)
  next index
  print
  print "The total is "; total
```

87

```
  print "The average is "; total / entryCount
end sub

[quit]
  end
```

Exercise One

Add code to ARRAYS.BAS after [quit] to display all the names entered.

Exercise Two

There's no reason we can't have more than one array in a BASIC program. For an example of this, look at the program file for FreeForm (it comes with Liberty BASIC). It uses dozens of arrays. Some of them are string arrays and some are of the numeric type. Modify the AVERAGE.BAS program so it asks for a name and age for up to 20 people. The names should be managed in a string array (remember ARRAYS.BAS?) that you'll add to the program. When the list of entries is displayed, each name is to be displayed with its age. Then the total and average age will be displayed after this. Call the program AGES.BAS.

Quiz - Answers on the next page

1) In programming, lists of data are managed using _____.

2) To set the size of an array, we use the _____ command.

3) The first item of an array has a position of _____.

4) A list managed by numeric position is an _____
_____.

5) Try to specify a position too big for an array and you will get an out of
_____ error.

6) Narrating the meaning of program code using intention revealing
subroutine names is called _____ _____.

7) In Liberty BASIC, arrays are _____ scoped.

Answers

1) arrays

2) DIM

3) 0 (zero)

4) indexed collection

5) bounds

6) composed factoring

7) globally

Chapter Seven

Reading and Writing Sequential Files - Part 1

Now we will learn about how to work with files. With some exceptions, modern personal computers store information as files on one or more hard disk drives. A personal computer may also have other storage devices which are mechanically different from a hard drive but which also keep files such as:

- Floppy drive (remember these?)
- CD/R or DVD/R
- Flash memory (CompactFlash, Secure Digital, etc.)
- USB drives (usually a form of flash memory)

Liberty BASIC provides ways to write information to files on these devices, and we can take advantage of this when we write our programs. Even though these different devices each have their own ways of keeping information in files, we can pretty much write the exact same code to work with files regardless of what kind of device they are stored on.

There are two ways to read and write files in Liberty BASIC. One way is called sequential and the other is called random access. In this chapter we will explain sequential files. The reason it is called sequential is that when reading or writing we start at the beginning of the file and work one item at a time to the end, in sequence. An item can be words or characters separated by commas, a numeric value represented by characters, or an item can be a complete line of data. It also also possible to write really fancy data using sequential files, such as sound, music or video, but that is *way* beyond the scope of this book.

Let's familiarize ourselves with a few Liberty BASIC commands that help us work with files.

OPEN

Let's say we want to work with a file named `myfile.txt`.

The OPEN command causes Liberty BASIC to open a file. A file must be opened if we want to write into it or read from it. There are several ways to open any file for sequential access. These ways are called modes.

The OUTPUT mode: The OUTPUT mode is for writing to a file. This is what an OPEN statement for OUTPUT looks like:

```
open "myfile.txt" for output as #myHandle
```

First, notice that we specify the file name myfile.txt. In order to open a file, we need to know its name (or you can make one up if it is a new file). Also, you can see the output mode is specified. The last item on the line is #myHandle. It is a name (called a file handle) given to Liberty BASIC to use for the open file. Any code that writes to this file must include a reference to #myHandle. This is so that Liberty BASIC knows which file to write to. Think of it as a shorthand or nickname for the file while it is open.

A file handle starts with a # character followed by any word or sequence of characters (using letters and digits). It is best to choose handles that make it easy for you to remember which file you are working with while writing your program. Some examples of valid file handles are:

```
#1
#abc
#dataFile
#customers
```

The INPUT mode: There is also a mode for reading sequentially from a file. This mode is called INPUT. Here is an example of an OPEN statement for INPUT:

```
open "myfile.txt" for input as #myHandle
```

If a file is opened with an input mode, be careful not to print any output to it or your program will stop with a runtime error.

CLOSE

The CLOSE statement is used for closing open files when we are done reading or writing them. This is a required operation when working with files and it is a very important thing to remember when writing programs.

Here is how OPEN and CLOSE work together:

```
open "myfile.txt" for output as #myHandle
'put some code in here that writes to #myHandle
close #myHandle
```

Another thing to remember is that a file opened for one mode must first be closed before it can be opened for a different mode. To read from a file you've just written to, you must close the file and reopen it, like so:

```
open "myfile.txt" for output as #myHandle
'put some code in here that writes to #myHandle
close #myHandle

open "myfile.txt" for input as #myHandle
'put some code in here that reads from #myHandle
close #myHandle
```

If you forget to close a file and then try to reopen it, your program will stop with an error.

PRINT

We've already seen how the PRINT statement can display text into a window on the screen. PRINT can also be used to write into a file opened for sequential OUTPUT. Here is an example:

```
open "myfile.txt" for output as #myHandle

print #myHandle, "Hello"
print #myHandle, "World!"
close #myHandle
```

This little program produces a file containing two lines of text (each could be considered an item, see above). Type the code in and run it. When the program finishes executing, open Windows Notepad on MYFILE.TXT to see the result!

You can open more than one file at a time. Perhaps you want to read information from a file, perform some kind of calculation on each line and as you go write the information to another file. If you do this, make sure that each file you open has its own handle (perhaps #reading and #writing in this case). If your program tries to open a file using a handle already used by another open file, your program will terminate with an error.

Let's Take It For A Spin

Now we'll modify the AGES.BAS program from the last chapter so that it saves the names and ages that we enter into a file. Take a look at this modified program:

```
'AGES-OUTPUT.BAS

'Accept names and ages, write them to a file,
'then total and average them.
dim person$(20)
dim age(20)
print "AGES-OUTPUT.BAS"
print
'loop up to 20 times, getting numbers
print "Enter up to 20 names and ages."
print "A zero or blank entry ends the series."

[entryLoop] 'loop until a zero entry or until index = 20
  'get a name
  print "Entry "; index + 1
  input "Person's name?"; personName$
  if personName$ = "" then [endSeries]
  input "Persons's age?"; entry$
  if entry$ = "" then [endSeries]
  entry = val(entry$)
  person$(index) = personName$   'set the name
  age(index) = entry   'set the age
  index = index + 1          'add one to index
  if index < 20 then [entryLoop]  'get another entry

[endSeries]   'entries are finished
  'Set entryCount to index
  entryCount = index
  if entryCount = 0 then print "No Entries." : end
  print "Entries completed."
  print
  print "Here are the "; entryCount; " entries:"
  print "----------------------------"
  for index = 0 to entryCount - 1
    print person$(index); " "; age(index)
  next index

  '*** New code starts here ***
  'Write the data into ages.dat
  open "ages.dat" for output as #ages
  for index = 1 to entryCount
    print #ages, person$(index)
    print #ages, age(index)
```

```
next index
close #ages
'*** New code ends here ***

'Now display the total and average value
for index = 0 to entryCount - 1
  total = total + age(index)
next index
print
print "The total is "; total
print "The average is "; total / entryCount

[quit]
  end
```

Type the new program lines in. Run the program and enter a few names and ages. When the program finishes executing, open the file with Notepad and you'll see the data you entered. It may look something like:

```
Tom Jones
52
Victor Krueger
39
Sue White
64
```

Let's see how our newly added code works.

1) First we open the file AGES.DAT with the OPEN statement. It is opened for OUTPUT (writing) and its file handle is #ages.

```
open "ages.dat" for output as #ages
```

2) Now we'll set up a FOR/NEXT loop.

```
for index = 1 to entryCount
```

3) Now we print a name and age, each on a separate line.

```
print #ages, person$(index)
print #ages, age(index)
```

4) Here's the back end of our FOR/NEXT loop. Loop back until index equals entryCount.

```
next index
```

5) Now we will close AGES.DAT.

```
close #ages
```

Reading from a file

Now that we've written information to a disk file, we are going to read that information back into our program. This is done using the INPUT statement. Just as we saw PRINT used to display information in a window and to write information to a disk file, INPUT can be used to get keyboard input, or to get information from a disk file.

To read from a file, it must be opened using the INPUT mode. The OPEN statement is used like so:

```
open "ages.dat" for input as #ages
```

Our INPUT statement for reading from a file looks a lot like the PRINT statement above:

```
input #ages, var$
```

Notice we use the file handle, and then we specify a variable name to read into. In a program that reads a list of items, an INPUT statement like the one above would be placed inside of a loop. In this way each item in the file can be read in turn and stored in an array.

An important point is that that we don't always know how many items have been written to AGES.DAT. This means we don't know when to stop looping around and reading items from the file. One solution is to add a PRINT statement to the program that creates the file. This PRINT statement would write the number of items at the start of the file, like so:

```
'Write the data into ages.dat
open "ages.dat" for output as #ages
print #ages, entryCount
for index = 1 to entryCount
  print #ages, person$(index)
  print #ages, age(index)
next index
close #ages
```

Then all we would need to do is read that number first, and then loop that many times to read each name and age. I will tackle it from a different direction though, because I want to introduce the EOF() function.

96

The EOF() function stands for End Of File. For a given file handle, it will return 0 if we are not at the end of file, and -1 if we are at the end of file. For example:

```
open "ages.dat" for input as #ages
if eof(#ages) = 0 then print "NOT AT END OF FILE"
close #ages
```

The above code would print NOT AT END OF FILE because we haven't read all the way to the end of the file.

Here is a version of AGES.BAS that reads it's information from the file we created above and uses EOF() to check for the end of file.

```
'AGES_INPUT.BAS
'Read names and ages from AGES.DAT totalling them.
'Compute and display the average age.
dim age(20)
dim person$(20)
print "AGES_IN.BAS"
print
print "Reading AGES.DAT..."
'open ages.dat
open "ages.dat" for input as #ages

'loop until end of file or index = 20
while eof(#ages) = 0 and index < 20
   'get the user's name and age
   input #ages, name$
   input #ages, age
   person$(index) = name$
   age(index) = age
   index = index + 1
   total = total + age
wend

[endSeries]  'entries are finished
  'close ages.dat
  close #ages
  if index = 0 then
    print "No Entries."
    goto [quit]
  end if
  'Set entryCount to index
  entryCount = index
  print "Entries completed."
  print
  print "Here are the "; entryCount; " entries:"
```

```
  print "----------------------------"
  'This loop displays each entered value in turn.
  'Notice that we re-use the index variable.  It
  'can be confusing to use a new variable for each
  'new loop.
  for index = 1 to entryCount
    print "Entry "; index; ": "; person$(index-1);
    print ", age "; age(index-1)
  next index
  'Now display the total and average value
  print
  print "The total age is "; total
  print "The average age is "; total / entryCount
[quit]
  end
```

Idea Break! - File Exists?

Sometimes it's necessary to make sure a file exists before you open it and read it. Do this using the FILES statement. For example:

```
'Show how to determine if a file exists
dim info$(10,10) 'You need the array
input "Type a file path (c:\folder\file.txt)"; fpath$
files path$(fpath$), filename$(fpath$), info$()
fileExists = val(info$(0, 0)) > 0
if not(fileExists) then
  print fpath$; " doesn't exist!"
end if
end

'get just the directory path from a full file path
function path$(fullPath$)
  path$ = fullPath$
  while right$(path$, 1) <> "\" and path$ <> ""
    path$ = left$(path$, len(path$)-1)
  wend
end function

'get just the filename from a full file path
function filename$(fullPath$)
  length = len(path$(fullPath$))
  filename$ = right$(fullPath$, len(fullPath$)-length)
end function
```

98

Exercise

Modify the program below so that it keeps its list in a disk file named ARRAYS.DAT. The program must read its list of names from ARRAYS.DAT before asking for additional names. When the user is done entering names, or if all the slots are filled, the list of names will be written to ARRAYS.DAT before the program ends. See the source code below for some clues.

```
'List handling with arrays and file input/output.
'This version stores more than 10 names.
dim names$(50)  'set up our array to contain 50 items

'*******
'Insert code here that reads ARRAYS.DAT into the
'array names$.
[askForName]  'ask for a name
  input "Please give me your name ?"; yourName$
  if yourName$ = "" then
    print "No name entered."
    goto [quit]
  end if

  index = 0
[insertLoop]
  'Does index point to an unused item in the array?
  if names$(index) = "" then
    names$(index) = yourName$
    goto [nameAdded]
  end if
  index = index + 1 'add 1 to index
  if index < 50 then [insertLoop]

  'There weren't any available slots, inform user
  print "All ten name slots already used!"
  goto [quit]

[nameAdded]  'Notify the name add was successful
  print yourName$; " has been added to the list."
  goto [askForName]

[quit]
  'display all the entered names
  print
  print "Here is a list of the names entered:"
  print "----------------------------------"
```

99

```
for index = 0 to 49
  if names$(index) <> "" then print names$(index)
next index

'****
'Insert code here to save the names$ array
'to the file ARRAYS.DAT

end
```

Quiz – Answers on the next page

1) In order to read or write a file, we must _____ it.

2) The OPEN command accepts INPUT or OUTPUT as _____.

3) To write to a file, we use the _____ command.

4) To read from a file, we use the _____ command.

5) When we are finished reading or writing, we use the _____ command.

6) The EOF() function tells us if we're at the _____ of _____.

7) If you try to open an already open file, Liberty BASIC will stop your program with an _____ message.

Answers

1) open

2) modes

3) PRINT

4) INPUT

5) CLOSE

6) end of file

7) error

Chapter Eight

Reading and Writing Sequential Files - Part 2

In the last section we covered the OUTPUT and INPUT file modes. These are for writing and reading files, respectively. This part of the lesson covers a new file mode called APPEND. We will also learn how to use the LINE INPUT command, and we will learn a few more new Liberty BASIC commands.

The APPEND file mode

There is a limitation in the OUTPUT file mode. The OUTPUT mode is only good for creating new files because it always deletes the contents of any file opened when it is used. For example:

```
'open a file and print some information into it
open "numbers.txt" for output as #numbers
for x = 1 to 10
  print #numbers, x
next x
close #numbers

'now rewrite the file, replacing its contents
open "numbers.txt" for output as #numbers
for x = 11 to 20
  print #numbers, x
next x
close #numbers
end
```

Run the above program and open Notepad on NUMBERS.TXT. You'll see that only the numbers 11 to 20 will be in the file. The only way to retain the original information in the file and add new information using the OUTPUT mode would be to read the original information and insert it into a new file. Then the new information is inserted into the still open file.

Here is what that code looks like:

```
'Open a file, and print some information into it
'then close it
open "numbers.txt" for output as #numbers
for x = 1 to 10
  print #numbers, x
next x
close #numbers

'open the original file for input
open "numbers.txt" for input as #in

'open the new file for output
open "numbers2.txt" for output as #numbers

[copyLoop] 'read from numbers.txt, write to numbers2.txt
  if eof(#in) then [doneCopying] 'end of numbers.txt
  input #in, value
  print #numbers, value
  goto [copyLoop]

[doneCopying]
  'close numbers.txt
  close #in
  'add more numbers to end of numbers2.txt
  for x = 11 to 20
    print #numbers, x
  next x
  close #numbers

  'Delete the original numbers.txt file and
  'rename numbers2.txt to numbers.txt.
  kill "numbers.txt"
  name "numbers2.txt" as "numbers.txt"
  end
```

Once the new file has been created containing the contents of the original file, plus our new numbers 11 to 20, we delete the old file using the KILL statement and rename the new file using the NAME statement.

There is a better way. Using the APPEND file mode, we can eliminate a lot of program code. The APPEND mode opens a file for writing, just like the OUTPUT mode does. Instead of erasing the contents of the file opened and starting at the beginning, the APPEND mode opens a file and retains everything. All we need to do then is write to the file, and everything we write will be added to the end of the file. Here is the example above

104

rewritten using the APPEND mode:

```
'Open a file and print some information into it,
'then close it
open "numbers.txt" for output as #numbers
for x = 1 to 10
  print #numbers, x
next x
close #numbers
'open the original file for append
open "numbers.txt" for append as #numbers
for x = 11 to 20
  print #numbers, x
next x
close #numbers
end
```

This is much shorter and simpler than the last example. When we are done writing the numbers 11 to 20 there is no need to delete or rename files.

Comma delimited files

By default, the standard way of reading from a sequential file using the INPUT statement breaks up the data we read at each end of line, and at each comma. Look at these equivalent file contents:

File 1 contents:

```
1,2,3,4,5,6,7,8,9,10
```

File 2 contents:

```
1,2,3,4,5
6,7,8,9,10
```

File 3 contents:

```
1
2
3
4
5
6
7
8
9
10
```

All three of the above possible file contents would produce the same displayed output using a loop like the following:

```
[loop]   'display each item on its own line
  while eof(#in) = 0
    input #in, item$   'read the next item
    print item$
  wend
```

Since the comma is used to separate items this kind of file format is often called *comma delimited* or *comma separated value* (with a file extension of .csv). This is a preferred generic format often used by commercial application software (spreadsheets are a good example) as a data export option. This is so that people like you and me can write our own customized software to use that information.

Idea Break! - Other Delimiters

Some files are not delimited using commas. Other popular delimiters are the Tab character (ASCII 9) and the | character, amongst others. Liberty BASIC can read such files by using the INPUTTO$( ) function:

```
'Read a Tab delimited file
tab$ = chr$(9)   'tab is ASCII 9
open "myfile.txt" for input as #readme
while eof(#readme) = 0
  item$ = inputto$(#readme, tab$)
  print "Next item: "; item$
wend
close #readme
```

LINE INPUT

What if we want to use commas in our information? As an example, we decide that we will build an application that logs responses to a direct mail campaign, and we want the name to be entered in a single field. The name will be entered last name first, with a comma separating the last from the

106

first name (example: Doe, John).

Take a look at this hypothetical file entry:

```
Doe, John
123 Main Street
Scottsdale
AZ
01234
```

Now look at this code fragment:

```
input #in, name$
input #in, street$
input #in, city$
input #in, state$
input #in, zip$
```

If we read the file entry with the above code, name$ would only contain up to the first comma. So name$ would contain the string "Doe", street$ would contain "John", city$ would contain "123 Main Street", and so on. This is not what we want.

There is a special form of the INPUT statement that will read a whole line from a file, including commas. It is the LINE INPUT statement. Here is the code fragment above rewritten using LINE INPUT:

```
line input #in, name$
line input #in, street$
line input #in, city$
line input #in, state$
line input #in, zip$
```

Another example of where LINE INPUT is useful is reading of a text document, like this one. There are many commas in this document. Here is a short program that uses the FILEDIALOG statement to ask for a *.txt file to read. Then it opens the file and reads and displays it.

```
'ask for a filename
filedialog "Select a text file", "*.TXT", filename$

'if filename$ = "" then the user canceled
if filename$ = "" then end

'open the file
open filename$ for input as #in
```

```
[readLoop]   'read and display each line in the text file
    if eof(#in) then [stopLooping]
    line input #in, lineOfText$
    print lineOfText$
    goto [readLoop]

[stopLooping]   'close the file
    close #in
    end
```

Run this small program and try it with a file that you know has some
commas in it. Then change the line containing the LINE INPUT statement
to use a regular INPUT statement and run the program again on the same
file so you can see how they function differently.

Here is what the FILEDIALOG statement produces on screen:

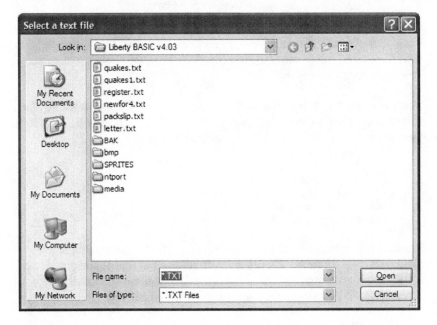

Exercise

Create a program called CALLER.BAS. This program will give the user
the following options:

1) Enter a phone call

2) Search by caller's name
3) Search by person called
3) Quit

Menu item 1 will ask the user for phone call information and append it as a new record to the end of a file named PHONELOG.TXT. The added record must include:

1) Caller's name
2) Name of person called
3) Date of the call
4) Time of the call
5) A one line description of the call's purpose
6) A phone # where the caller can be reached

When searching, the program should stop and display the six data items for each record that matches and ask if the user wants to keep searching or quit the search. The program will display a notice if no matches are found.

Possible enhancement to CALLER.BAS

It is possible to search for a partial match. Look at the following code:

```
text$ = "The quick brown fox jumped over the lazy dog."
searchFor$ = "FOX"
print "Searching for:"
print "  "; searchFor$
print "In the following:"
print "  "; text$
a$ = upper$(text$)
b$ = upper$(searchFor$)
if instr(a$, b$) > 0 then
    print "Found!"
else
    print "Not Found!"
end if
```

The UPPER$() function eliminates any letter case differences. The INSTR() function returns a 0 value if our uppercased searchFor$ is not found in our uppercased text, or it returns the position of searchFor$ if it is found.

Try changing the value of searchFor$ from "FOX" to other values and re-run the program.

Quiz – Answers are on the next page

1) To open a sequential file so that you can add new information to the end of the file, use the _____ mode.

2) If we need to search for one string inside of another we can use the _____ function.

3) To read each data item in a comma delimited file, use the _____ statement.

4) To change the name of a file, use the _____ statement.

5) A file that separates data with commas (ie. 50, 34, 98, 101) is called a _____ _____ file.

6) To delete a file, use the _____ statement.

7) To read whole lines from a file including the commas we can use the _____ _____ statement.

8) The _____ statement pops up a window for choosing a file.

Answers

1) APPEND

2) INSTR( )

3) INPUT

4) NAME

5) comma delimited

6) KILL

7) LINE INPUT

8) FILEDIALOG

Chapter Nine

Programming the Windows Graphical User Interface

What is a GUI (graphical user interface) anyway? This probably means different things to different people but to most it means a way of controlling a computer that involves manipulating windows (rectangular areas displayed on a computer screen) using a mouse or other pointing device.

If you are using Microsoft WINDOWS then you are using a software system with a GUI (we will use all uppercase when referring to Microsoft's product and not to any kind of window in general). WINDOWS is an operating system that includes a GUI.

You have been using the WINDOWS GUI all along while working through this Liberty BASIC course. The programs that you've written each run in a window that is managed by the WINDOWS GUI. This simple text-only window is called a *main window* in Liberty BASIC lingo. This part of the course will teach you how to add fancier GUI features to your programs.

In this section we will learn:

1) How to use Liberty BASIC to open windows in the WINDOWS GUI
2) How to set the size, position, and type of our windows
3) How to add buttons and other controls to our windows
4) How to program the buttons and other controls to do what we want

Your First Window!

Type in the following short program and run it. Insert your name in the place where it says myname.

```
'show them the main window
print "I'm the main window!"

'open another window
```

113

```
open "myname's first window!" for window as #myFirst
'now stop and wait
wait
end
```

Two windows will appear. One is the main window (we've been using this kind of window all along). The other window will appear with your name in the title! That was easy, wasn't it? Now click on the program's initial window (called its *main window*). Now close this window and the program will end.

Liberty BASIC uses file statements like OPEN, CLOSE and PRINT to manage and control windows. Once a window is opened, we can send it commands by PRINTing to it.

Note: There is nothing to prevent a Liberty BASIC program from opening more than one window as demonstrated. All you need is multiple OPEN statements, and each window must have a unique handle (the window in the example above has the handle #myFirst).

We don't have to use a string literal when setting the title of a window we open. Here is a slightly fancier example:

```
'ask for a name
input "What's your name bud?"; you$

'open a window
open you$+"'s first window!" for window as #fancy

'now stop and wait
wait
end
```

Adjusting Window Size and Position

Let's change the size of our Window. This is done by changing the value of two special variables WindowWidth and WindowHeight before opening the window. We can also determine the opening position of the window by adjusting two other special variables UpperLeftX and UpperLeftY. This positioning is relative to the upper-left corner of the display screen. Take a look at this example:

```
'open a window sized 300x100 at position 200, 150
WindowWidth = 300
WindowHeight = 100
UpperLeftX = 200
UpperLeftY = 150
open "I have custom size!" for window as #sized

'now stop and wait
wait
end
```

Adding a button

Now let's add a button to our window. Look at the following short program:

```
'open a window with a button
'the window is sized at 300 by 100 at position 200, 150

WindowWidth = 300
WindowHeight = 100
UpperLeftX = 200
UpperLeftY = 150
button #myFirst.ok, "OK!", [okClicked], UL, 15, 15
open "myname's first window!" for window as #myFirst

'now stop and wait
wait

[okClicked]  'the OK! button was clicked
  notice "You clicked on OK!"

[quit]
  'now close the window
  close #myFirst

  end
```

Notice the BUTTON statement we placed before the OPEN statement. This must be inserted *before* the OPEN statement. Let's break that line of code down to explain how it works.

```
button #myFirst.ok, "OK!", [okClicked], UL, 15, 15
```

The first item in the BUTTON statement is a handle for the button. In this case our handle is #myFirst.ok. We are adding this button to a window

115

that will have a handle of #myFirst, and we add .ok to extend the handle so that the button will have its own handle different from the handle of the window.

The second item "OK!" is the button caption.

The third item is the [okClicked] branch label. This tells Liberty BASIC to perform an implicit GOTO [okClicked] when the button is clicked on. In this case the NOTICE statement causes a dialog box to appear that displays "You clicked on OK!". Once you close the dialog box the window will be closed and the program will end.

The fourth item (UL) tells Liberty BASIC that the button will be positioned relative to the upper-left corner of the window. There are also UR, LL, and LR (for placing buttons relative to the upper-right, lower-left and lower-right corners).

The fifth and sixth items specify how many pixels from the (in this case upper-left) corner to place the button.

One option is to specify the exact width and height of the button. Liberty BASIC automatically chooses the size of the button if you don't specify it. Here's the same button, but we'll change the size to 75 pixels wide and 50 pixels high:

```
    button #myFirst.ok, "OK!", [okClicked], UL, 15, 15,
75, 50
```

The WAIT statement in our program is very important. Liberty BASIC will react to user actions performed on buttons or other controls when a running program is stopped at a WAIT statement (also SCAN and INPUT statements, but we won't cover those here).

Controls

Buttons and other things that are added to a GUI window for a user to click on or type into are commonly called controls because they are used to control the program. Other terms programmers use for the concept of a control include widget, component, and object (but object also has very broad meaning in computer programming).

Adding an Entry Field with TEXTBOX

Now let's add a textbox control to our window that let's us display and edit a line of text. We will use the TEXTBOX statement to accomplish this. Look at this code:

```
'open a window with a button and a textbox
'the window is sized at 300 by 100 at position 200, 150
WindowWidth = 300
WindowHeight = 100
UpperLeftX = 200
UpperLeftY = 150
button #myFirst.ok, "OK!", [okClicked], UL, 15, 15
textbox #myFirst.field, 60, 15, 200, 25
open "myname's first window!" for window as #myFirst

'now print some text into the textbox
print #myFirst.field, "Type some text here."

'now stop and wait
wait

[okClicked]   'OK! was clicked.
   'now get the contents from the textbox
   print #myFirst.field, "!contents? aString$"

   'now pop up a notice saying what was in the textbox
   notice aString$

[quit]
   'now close the window
   close #myFirst

   end
```

Run the example and see how it works! Notice the TEXTBOX statement after the BUTTON statement. Its format is very simple.

```
textbox #myFirst.field, 60, 15, 200, 25
```

The first item #myFirst.field is a handle for the textbox. This is just like the handle we gave to our button.

The next two items 60 and 15 are the placement of the control relative to the upper-left corner of the window.

The last two items 200 and 25 are the width and height of the control. Note: If it isn't tall enough, you won't see any text in the control at all.

After our OPEN statement, see how we print some text "Type some text here." into our textbox control. This is the text that you see in the control when the program is run.

Now look at how we changed the code after our [okClicked] branch label. Instead of just displaying the same message every time it displays the text in our textbox control. We accomplish this by printing a command to the textbox with the line:

```
print #myFirst.field, "!contents? aString$"
```

This tells Liberty BASIC that we want to put the contents of that textbox control into the variable named aString$. We could also have written this as two separate PRINT and INPUT statements as follows, and you may see other Liberty BASIC programs which do it this way:

```
print #myFirst.field, "!contents?"
input #myFirst.field, aString$
```

When printing a command to a textbox control, the command must start with an exclamation point. This is how Liberty BASIC knows that we want to send a command to the textbox. The contents of our textbox would have been replaced with "contents? aString$" if we had left out the exclamation point like so:

```
'this would not work
print #myFirst.field, "contents? aString$"
```

Labeling with Statictext Controls

So far our window designs have been simple enough that we haven't needed to mark any part of our window with a descriptive label or annotation. This is an important matter in many applications where more than one textbox (or other kind of control) is used. Here is a version of our program that uses a statictext control as a label:

```
'open a window with a button, a textbox, and a statictext
'the window is sized at 300 by 100 at position 200, 150
WindowWidth = 300
WindowHeight = 100
UpperLeftX = 200
UpperLeftY = 150
button #myFirst.ok, "OK!", [okClicked], UL, 220, 35
textbox #myFirst.field, 10, 35, 200, 25
statictext #myFirst.label, "Type some text", 10, 10, 150, 25
open "myname's first window!" for window as #myFirst

'now stop and wait
wait

[okClicked]   'OK! was clicked.

'now get the contents from the textbox
print #myFirst.field, "!contents? aString$"

'now pop up a notice saying what was in the textbox
notice aString$

[quit]
'now close the window
close #myFirst

end
```

See how we move the button and the textbox around in the window, and we add a text description with instructions to the user. The format for the STATICTEXT statement is almost the same as for the TEXTBOX statement.

```
statictext #myFirst.label, "Type some text", 10, 10, 150, 25
```

The first item is a string used for the text in our statictext control.

The second item #myFirst.label is a handle for the statictext. This is just like the handle we gave to our button.

The text within the quote marks is the caption for the control.

The next two items 10 and 10 are the placement of the control relative to the upper-left corner of the window.

The last two items 150 and 25 are the width and height of the control. The size must be large enough to hold the text. If it isn't wide enough, the end of the line will not appear. If it isn't tall enough, you won't see any text in the control at all.

Trapping a Window Close Event

When running any of our examples above we can close our custom made window at any time by double-clicking on its menu box, by pressing Alt-F4, etc. Then WINDOWS will go ahead and close the window, but Liberty BASIC will still think it's open. This will cause some trouble if our code tries to perform some work with a window that just isn't there anymore.

The way around this problem is by sending the trapclose command to our window in question. The trapclose command tells Liberty BASIC to hook into the WINDOWS event that closes our window. Here is our program modified to use trapclose.

```
'open a window with a button, a textbox, and a statictext
'show how trapclose works
'the window is sized at 300 by 100 at position 200, 150
WindowWidth = 300
WindowHeight = 100
UpperLeftX = 200
UpperLeftY = 150
button #myFirst.ok, "OK!", [okClicked], UL, 220, 35
textbox #myFirst.field, 10, 35, 200, 25
statictext #myFirst.label, "Type some text", 10, 10, 150, 25
open "myname's first window!" for window as #myFirst

'send the trapclose command
print #myFirst, "trapclose [quit]"

'now stop and wait
wait

[okClicked]   'OK! was clicked.

'now get the contents from the textbox
print #myFirst.field, "!contents? aString$"

'now pop up a notice saying what was in the textbox
notice aString$

[quit]
'ask if the user wants to quit
confirm "Really Quit?"; answer$
if answer$ <> "yes" then wait 'abort quitting
```

120

```
'now close the window
close #myFirst

end
```

See how the trapclose command that we print to our window also specifies the [quit] branch label. This means that when we try to close the window using a mouse or keyboard action (using the CLOSE statement doesn't trigger trapclose), then WINDOWS will not close the window. Instead Liberty BASIC will execute a GOTO [quit].

Notice also how we added code following the [quit] branch label. Using a CONFIRM statement the program pops up a dialog box to ask whether to quit. If the user answers no, the program executes a WAIT statement. Once this happens then the program ready for the user to do something else.

Exercise

We can add many controls to a window in Liberty BASIC. If we need a dozen textboxes to hold different data items and if we need a statictext to label each textbox we can do it. Create a program that opens a window titled "Caller Record Data". This window contains several textbox controls, each labeled by a statictext control. Here is the list of information the window should collect from the user:

1) Caller's name
2) Name of person called
3) Date
4) Time of call
5) Purpose of call
6) Caller can be reached at

When the user clicks on OK!, the program should then extract all the information entered into the textbox controls and print it to the program's main window.

Quiz – Answers on the next page

1) To create and display a window use the _____ statement and the _____ mode.

2) To cause a program to wait for a user to interact with a window we use the _____ statement.

3) Add a button to a window with the _____ statement.

4) To control the size and position of a window when it opens we use the special variables _____ , _____ , _____ , and _____ .

5) Buttons, textboxes and other things added to a window are called _____ .

6) Control statements must occur before the _____ statement for a window.

7) Add a box for text entry to a window using the _____ statement.

8) Create a label on a window using the _____ statement.

9) Each control on a window must have a unique _____ .

10) A good handle for an OK button on a window which has the handle #application would be _____ .

11) Use the _____ window command add a handler for closing a window.

12) To popup a window with a Yes/No question use the _____ statement.

Answers

1) OPEN, WINDOW

2) WAIT

3) BUTTON

4) WindowHeight, WindowWidth, UpperLeftX, UpperLeftY

5) controls

6) OPEN

7) TEXTBOX

8) STATICTEXT

9) handle

10) #application.ok

11) trapclose

12) CONFIRM

Chapter Ten

More Programming the Graphical User Interface

Adding Menus to a Window

We've shown how to add buttons to windows so that the user can invoke actions. We can also add pull-down menus to our programs. These include the common File, Edit, View, Help, etc. menus. You can add dozens of user actions to a window with menus, but just try adding dozens of buttons to a window. You wouldn't have room for anything else!

Just look at this simple example:

```
'lunch today
label$ = "Your selection: "
menu #main, "&Lunch Specials", _
    "&Scrod soup", [scrod], _
    "&Haggis", [haggis], _
    "&Mud Pie", [mudPie]
statictext #main.choice, label$, 10, 10, 250, 30
open "May I help you?" for window as #main
#main "trapclose [quit]"
wait

[scrod]
  #main.choice label$ + "Scrod soup?  What's that?"
  wait

[haggis]
  #main.choice label$ + "Stuffed sheep stomach, Oy!"
  wait

[mudPie]
  #main.choice label$ + "Mud pie looks like fudge!"
  wait

[quit]
  close #main
  end
```

125

Note: Right at the beginning of the code that we use the underscore to break up the MENU command in our example. Menus that have more than a couple of items tend to get pretty long, so using the underscore to break them up over several lines is useful. The underscore can be used to split up any command into several lines to make it more readable.

Just like the commands for adding other kinds of controls like buttons and textboxes, the MENU command must come before the window is opened.

The menu has a title 'Lunch Specials', and three items named Scrod, Haggis, and Mud Pie. Each of these items has a branch label to jump to. Also see the ampersand & characters. These give the letter following them special *accelerator* status. To invoke a menu item using accelerators, use the Alt key and the indicated letter in the menu title (Alt+L in the example). This causes the menu to appear on screen. Then find the desired menu action item and press the underline letter on the keyboard. So for scrod soup, press Alt+L and then S.

You can have more than one menu. Right after the first MENU command we could add a second menu to our example program that might look something like:

```
menu #main, "&Food Alert", _
    "&Head for the hills", [headForHills], _
    "&Slip the food to the dog", [feedDog], _
    "&Feed parking meter excuse", [parkingMeter] _
    "&Dial 911", [dial911]
```

Another thing we can do it add separators between items in the menu. This is a visual cue that groups related menu items together. We do this by putting a | (on most keyboards this is Shift+\) between items in the menu command. Try substituting the following menu command in the example program above. Run it to see what this looks like:

```
menu #main, "&Lunch Specials", _
    "&Scrod soup", [scrod], _
    |, _
    "&Haggis", [haggis], _
    "&Mud Pie", [mudPie]
```

126

Idea Break! - Accelerated Buttons

Just as we can use accelerators with menus we can also do this with buttons. All we need to do it use the ampersand & character in our BUTTON statement:

```
button #main.button1,"&Go",[go], UL, 0, 0, 105, 25
open "untitled" for window as #main
print #main, "font ms_sans_serif 10"
wait

[go]
  notice "Tada!"
  wait
```

Run the example and then press Alt+G to popup the Tada! notice.

Using NOMAINWIN

The default text window that opens with each Liberty BASIC program we create can be optionally turned off. This can be desirable when we don't want our application to be operated out of a text window. The command that accomplishes this effect is NOMAINWIN. Simply include NOMAINWIN in your program's source code anywhere at all. This accomplishes two things:

1) It hides the program's main window;
2) It prevents the 'Execution Complete' notice from appearing at the end of a program run.

This comes at a cost. Your program must close itself down properly when all the windows have been closed. Check out the example below.

```
'demonstrate the NOMAINWIN command
'the window is sized at 300 by 100
nomainwin  'do not open a main window
WindowWidth = 300
WindowHeight = 100
button #example.ok, "OK!", [okClicked], UL, 220, 35
```

127

```
textbox #example.field, 10, 35, 200, 25
statictext #example.label, "Type something", 10, 10, 150, 25
open "myname's first window!" for window as #example
#example "trapclose [quit]"
wait   'stop and wait for user interaction

[okClicked]  'Get the contents of the entry field
  'now get the contents from the textbox
  #example.field "!contents? aString$"
  'now pop up a notice saying what was in the textbox
  notice aString$
  wait   'stop and wait for user interaction

[quit]
  'ask if the user wants to quit
  confirm "Really Quit?"; answer$
  if answer$ <> "yes" then wait 'abort quitting
  'now close the window
  close #example
  end
```

After the CLOSE #example statement in our program above, we have an
END statement. If we didn't, then our program would not terminate
properly, and there would be no error message to clue us in. Always use
END in your programs because just closing all the windows doesn't end
the program. There are kinds of programs which don't have windows open
all the time, and even some which don't have any windows at all.

Here's what the program looks like when it runs:

Note: If you hide the main window with NOMAINWIN, you can still
PRINT to it. The output will go into limbo (nowhere). Even if your

128

program doesn't need a main window, this can be a really handy way to log debugging commentary. When the program runs to your satisfaction, put a NOMAINWIN command in there to hide the debugging log. Then if the extra invisible PRINT commands make your program run too slowly, remove them.

The Structure of a Liberty BASIC GUI Program

We've taken a look at some simple elements of Liberty BASIC GUI programming. Now let's consider how to factor code in a logical and practical way when creating GUI programs in LB.

Organization

In the case of a project that uses more than one window, we should make sure that code for each window is grouped together. Most applications are designed around a central window that is always open and from where other windows are launched. When the central window is closed, the application ends. Liberty BASIC is a good example of this kind of structure. When you start it up the Liberty BASIC editor appears. From there you can open some other windows for opening and saving files, for setting preferences and more. Until you close the Liberty BASIC editor, Liberty BASIC continues to run.

Here is an outline (not a working program) that demonstrates this idea:

```
'This is an example outline
'--Define our main application window here
button #main.1, ....
button #main.2, ....
textbox ....
open "My Application" for window as #main
#main "trapclose [closeMain]"
wait  'stop and wait for user action

[button1Clicked]
  'do something here for button1
  wait

[button2Clicked]
  'do something here for button2
  wait
```

```
[closeMain]  'perform cleanup code and close the window
  close #main
  gosub [sub1]  'act on user action

  'end application
  end

[openWin2]   '--Define our second window here
  button #2.3, ....
  button #2.4, ....
  textbox ....
  open "Window 2" for window as #2
  #2 "trapclose [close2]"
  wait  'stop and wait here for user action

[button3Clicked]
  'do something here for button3
  wait

[button4Clicked]
  'do something here for button4
  wait

[close2]  'perform some cleanup code and close the window
  close #2
  gosub [sub2]  'act on user action
  wait


'--------------------------------------------------
  'We might place code here containing
  'general subroutines
```

See how we arrange the code for each window like so:

```
[openMainWindow]
[userAction1]
[userAction2]
[closeMainWindow]
     end

[openWindow1]
[userAction3]
[userAction4]
[closeWindow1]

[openWindow2]
[userAction5]
[userAction6]
[closeWindow2]
```

The names we give to our branch labels above are of course generic. All the code for a given window and user actions performed on it should be grouped together. By structuring things in this way it is relatively easy to develop and debug your programs.

NOTE: Be careful to avoid creating a program that closes all its windows but doesn't actually end. If the program stops at an input or wait statement after closing all of it's windows, it will not terminate properly and resources will not be freed. If the program loops continuously after closing all its windows then Liberty BASIC's WINDOWS message handler will be locked out. In this case press CTRL-Break to halt the errant program, then use the Kill BASIC Programs item from the Liberty BASIC Run menu to clean up the program.

Using SUBs for User Event Handlers

So far we have showed how to specify handlers using branch labels such as [okClicked] and [quit]. When we covered the use of the SUB statement back in chapter 5 we also explained that using SUBs and FUNCTIONs is preferable to code using branch labels because they have stronger scoping. This makes it easier to keep the different parts of your program untangled.

We can take advantage of the benefits of SUBs when we use controls. Instead of specifying the name of a branch label when we add a control we specify the name of a SUB. Here is the NOMAINWIN example from a few pages ago rewritten to show how this works:

```
'demonstrate the NOMAINWIN command
'the window is sized at 300 by 100
nomainwin  'do not open a main window
WindowWidth = 300
WindowHeight = 100
button #example.ok, "OK!", okClicked, UL, 220, 35
textbox #example.field, 10, 35, 200, 25
statictext #example.label, "Type something", 10, 10, 150, 25
open "myname's first window!" for window as #example
#example "trapclose quit"
wait    'stop and wait for user interaction

sub okClicked handle$  'Get the contents of the entry field
  'now get the contents from the textbox
  #example.field "!contents? aString$"
```

131

```
   'now pop up a notice saying what was in the textbox
   notice aString$
end sub    'stop and wait for user interaction

sub quit handle$
  'ask if the user wants to quit
  confirm "Really Quit?"; answer$
  if answer$ <> "yes" then wait 'abort quitting
  'now close the window
  close #example
  end
end sub
```

Notice there is no WAIT statement at the end of the okClicked handler. When execution reaches the `end sub` it does the same thing as WAIT.

When you use a SUB for an event handler, any variables that you need to access from inside that handler must be declared global. For example:

```
'counter1.bas
textbox #counter.tb, 10, 10, 50, 25
button #counter.add, "+", [add], UL, 70, 10, 30, 25
button #counter.subtract, "-", [subtract], UL, 110,10,30,25
open "Counter 1" for window as #counter
#counter.tb count
wait

[add]
  count = count + 1
  #counter.tb count
  wait

[subtract]
  count = count - 1
  #counter.tb count
  wait
```

Here is a version using SUBs for event handlers. The count variable must be declared global. If it isn't then the value of count will be initialized to zero each time the event handlers are activated.

```
'counter2.bas
global count
textbox #counter.tb, 10, 10, 50, 25
button #counter.add, "+", add, UL, 70, 10, 30, 25
button #counter.subtr, "-", subtr, UL, 110, 10, 30, 25
open "Counter 1" for window as #counter
#counter.tb count
wait

sub add control$
  count = count + 1
  #counter.tb count
end sub

sub subtr control$
  count = count - 1
  #counter.tb count
end sub
```

How do you think the program will behave if the global count statement is removed from the beginning of the program? Try it and see.

Notice the control$ variable in the SUB statement? This contains the name of the control that caused the handler to be executed. This can be very handy so that one handler can perform different tasks depending on which control was used.

Here is a simple example of how this works:

```
'UpperLower.bas
textbox #demo.tb, 10, 10, 200, 100
button #demo.upper, "Upper", process, UL, 10, 120, 30, 25
button #demo.lower, "Lower", process, UL, 10, 50, 30, 25
open "Two buttons" for window as #demo
#demo.tb "Try Clicking Upper and Lower!"
wait

sub process control$
  text$ = #demo.tb "!contents?"
  if control$ = "#demo.upper" then
      #demo.tb upper$(text$)
  end if
  if control$ = "#demo.lower" then
      #demo.tb lower$(text$)
  end if
end sub
```

The user is presented with a text area containing the string *Try Clicking*

Upper and Lower! Then clicking Upper changes the text to all uppercase, and clicking Lower changes the text to all lowercase. Both buttons use the same SUB to handle the button being clicked. That handler tests the control$ variable to see which button was clicked and then uses either UPPER$( ) or LOWER$( ) appropriately.

Using Dialog Boxes

Dialog boxes are a special kind of window. They are different in several respects from other windows:

1) Dialog boxes can be made modal. This means that if I have a first window open and then I open a modal dialog box, that I will be unable to select the first window until the modal dialog is closed. Most 'About' boxes are modal dialogs, as are many 'Properties' type windows. For an example, select Liberty BASIC's Help menu and click on 'About Liberty BASIC'. You won't be able to do anything else with Liberty BASIC until you close the dialog box that appears.

2) Dialog boxes cannot be resized by the user, and they don't have minimize or maximize buttons.

3) Dialog boxes can have a *default pushbutton* which is activated when the use presses the Enter key. Most of the time a dialog box's default pushbutton is the OK or Accept button.

4) Dialog boxes cannot have pull-down menus.

Some applications are appropriately constructed completely of dialog boxes and have no other kind of window at all. Take a look at the program FreeForm which comes with Liberty BASIC. This program is more typical. The main application windows is a graphics type, but most of the other windows are dialog boxes.

More About Statictext

We saw in the first part of this lesson how a statictext control is used to label other controls in a window. Statictext controls do not have to display the same label all the time. We can print to them in similar fashion to the way we print to a textbox control. Try the example code below:

```
'demonstrate printing to statictext control
nomainwin
statictext #main.statictext, "Countdown:", 10, 10, 200, 25
open "Countdown" for window as #main
#main "trapclose [quit]"
for count = 10 to 1 step -1
  #main.statictext "Countdown: "; count
  t$ = time$()
  while t$ = time$()   'loop until the time changes
  wend
next count
#main.statictext "Countdown: Done."
wait
[quit]
  close #main
  end
```

Since we can change the contents of a statictext control, it isn't really static. Pesky little thing isn't it? ;-)

Exercise - HILO Revisited

Create a version of the HILO program using the techniques in this lesson. The program should have its own application window using the window type. This window should have at least one statictext control. One of these should indicate whether to guess higher or lower and to count the guesses. There should be a textbox for entering guesses, and a button labeled 'Guess' to click on to register each guess. An additional button should be labeled 'About'. This button should cause an About box to be displayed for the game. The About box should be constructed as a modal dialog box using an OPEN command similar to:

```
'this would be just part of a larger program
WindowWidth = 160
WindowHeight = 100
statictext #about, "I am an example about box", 10, 10,
150, 25
button #about.ok, "OK", [closeAbout], UL,  50, 40, 50,
25
open "My About Box" for dialog_modal as #about
#about "trapclose [closeAbout]"
wait

[closeAbout]
close #about
```

In addition to the buttons, add a menu titled 'Play' with two action items called 'Guess' and 'Exit'. Guess should perform the same action as clicking in the Guess button, and Exit should cause the game to quit. Add a second menu titled 'Help' with one action item called 'About HILO' which performs the same action as clicking the About button.

Quiz - Answers on the next page

1) Use the ampersand character to add _____ to menus.

2) Dialog boxes can be made _____, but regular windows cannot.

3) Users cannot _____ dialog boxes.

4) To hide the main window, use the _____ command.

5) When quitting your program, make sure to use an _____ command after closing all the windows to make sure the program terminates properly.

6) To change the contents of a statictext control we _____ to it.

7) Only dialog boxes can have a _____ pushbutton.

8) _____ _____ cannot have pulldown menus.

9) Press Ctrl+Break to stop a program that is _____ out of control.

10) SUBs can be used as _____ handlers for user actions.

11) Use the GLOBAL statement to make variables visible inside of _____.

12) A SUB is passed a string with the name of the _____ of the control that invoked the SUB, for example:

```
sub clickHandler handleName$
    print "you clicked on the control: "; handleName$
end sub
```

13) Use one or more _____ to split a line of code into more than one line.

Answers

1) accelerators

2) modal

3) resize

4) NOMAINWIN

5) END

6) PRINT

7) default

8) dialog boxes

9) running

10) event

11) SUBs

12) handle

13) underscores

Chapter Eleven

Drawing Graphics with Liberty BASIC

One of the things computers are most famous for is the creation of fancy images, also known as computer graphics. Liberty BASIC has a lot of commands for doing this sort of thing, and here we're going to give you the grand tour.

Virtual Canvas

Just like in the real world an artist will paint on a canvas (usually anyways), Liberty BASIC has a special place for drawing graphics. You can open a whole window for drawing graphics. Let's make a virtual Picasso painting:

```
open "Paint a Picasso" for graphics as #picasso
#picasso "trapclose [quit]"

#picasso "down"
#picasso "home"

'draw the head
#picasso "backcolor cyan ; ellipsefilled 120 200"

'draw the nose
#picasso "size 8"
#picasso "place 120 100"
#picasso "goto 90 130 ; goto 120 140"

'draw the eye
#picasso "place 160 100"
#picasso "color red"
#picasso "circle 15"

'draw the mouth
#picasso "color green"
#picasso "place 110 200"
#picasso "goto 120 190 ; goto 160 220"

'make it all stick
#picasso "flush"
```

```
      wait

[quit]
      close #picasso
      end
```

Here is what Liberty BASIC will draw when you run it.

This is no great work of art, but it does look sort of like a Picasso,
right? ;-) Not pretty, but perfect for demonstrating the basics of drawing
graphics in Liberty BASIC.

The first couple of lines should look familiar. We use this precise kind of
code to open windows in the last lesson.

```
      open "Paint a Picasso" for graphics as #picasso
      #picasso "trapclose [quit]"
```

See that we open the window as a graphics type. Then we set up a
trapclose handler.

```
      #picasso "down"
      #picasso "home"
```

Now we send a couple of commands to the graphics window. Liberty
BASIC graphics use a virtual pen with which we draw our graphics. Just

like a real pen, we can put the pen down in order to draw, or we can pick it up (that command is called up). Unless we put the pen down, any drawing commands we use will not have any visible effect.

The home command simply puts the pen in the center of the graphics window.

```
'draw the head
#picasso "backcolor cyan ; ellipsefilled 120 200"
```

Now we want to draw a head. We want to set a color for the head. When you want to draw a filled shape, the backcolor command is used to set the fill color. As appropriate for the strange theme of a Picasso portrait, we choose the cyan color because it's just so strange. We will pick some more weird colors as we go.

Now, after the backcolor command, we have another command in the same string. We can do this just by separating them with a ; (a semicolon) character. This let's us save some lines of code. If we didn't use the semicolon it would take two lines, like so:

```
#picasso "backcolor cyan"
#picasso "ellipsefilled 120 200"
```

When do we use a semicolon? This is up to the programmer. Some people never use it, and some like to use it a lot.

After the ; we put an ellipsefilled command. This draws an ellipse (like an oval) 120 pixels wide and 200 pixels high. A *pixel* is what we call each of the little dots that make up a computer display. The term is short for *picture element*.

Let's draw a nose:

```
'draw the nose
#picasso "size 8"
#picasso "place 120 100"
#picasso "goto 90 130 ; goto 120 140"
```

So that we can use a broad stroke, we set the size of the pen. The pen is set to a size of 1 unless we change it. Let's put the pen somewhere so we can begin a drawing stroke of the pen.

141

The place command moves the pen to position 120 and 100. These numbers are always measured in pixels, and always from the upper left of the window. *This part is a little strange, but computer graphics positions are almost always measured from the upper left, probably because this is the corner where a television display tube begins drawing.* So we put the pen 120 pixels from the left and 100 pixels from the top of the window.

Now we use the goto command (not the same as a GOTO [branchLabel]). This tells the pen to go from its current position to the specified position, drawing all the way (because the pen is down). Going from 120, 100 to 90, 130 makes a fat line going down and left. Then the second goto command draws a line to 120, 140 (down and right).

A nice nose! :-)

Okay, now we will draw an eye.

```
'draw the eye
#picasso "place 160 100"
#picasso "color red"
#picasso "circle 15"
```

Again, we use the place command to put the pen where we would like to draw the eye. Now we want a red eye (hey, why not?) so we use the color command. We used the backcolor command before when we wanted to specify the fill color of the head, but now we use the color command to specify the color of the border color. Now when we use the circle command, we draw a circle with a radius of 15 and the border is red.

What's a face without a mouth? Let's add one:

```
'draw the mouth
#picasso "color green"
#picasso "place 110 200"
#picasso "goto 120 190 ; goto 160 220"
```

First, the color command is used to set the color of the pen to green. Now we do just exactly what we did when we drew the nose. The place command sets us up for drawing the mouth at position 110, 200. Then we use two goto commands to draw the mouth.

142

Drawing text using graphics

Now for the finishing touch. Let's add a title to our painting:

```
'add a title
#picasso "color blue"
#picasso "place 100 280"
#picasso "\Mama Pajama"
```

First our old friend the color command makes our title blue. Then we place the pen at the bottom of our portrait. The last line uses a \ to tell the graphics window to draw Mama Pajama at the pen location.

Now, one final thing we do after drawing all that stuff is to tell the graphics window to make it *stick*. The flush command puts all the drawn graphics into a *drawing segment*. In effect this makes the drawing operations into a single object so they can be managed together.

```
'make it all stick
#picasso "flush"
wait
```

The most immediate benefit of using flush is that the drawn graphics will be redrawn correctly if the window is covered by another window and then uncovered, when the scrollbars are used to move the graphics around, or if the window is minimized and restored. Run the program and try one or more of the above. The graphics will automatically redraw when needed. Try commenting out the `#picasso "flush"` line and then run it again. The graphics will not automatically be redrawn. There are other useful things about flush which we will cover later.

Finally, we have a rather standard trapclose handler as shown here:

```
[quit]
  close #picasso
  end
```

Once you've drawn some graphics, you can send those graphics to
your printer using the print graphics command. Here is a really simple
example:

```
'send some graphics to the printer
open "Printer Graphics" for graphics as #draw
#draw "down"
for x = 1 to 300 step 10
  #draw "line "; x; " 0 "; 300 - x; " 200"
next x
#draw "place 120 100"
#draw "\warp drive!"
#draw "print"
wait
```

Graphics in a non graphics window

You can draw graphics in a window that isn't a graphics window. This is
simply a matter of adding a graphicbox control to a window or dialog box.
Here is our Picasso program that uses a graphicbox instead of a graphics
window.

```
'specify the size of the window
WindowWidth = 300
WindowHeight = 330

'set up a graphicbox
graphicbox #main.picasso, 4, 4, 260, 280
open "Paint a Picasso" for window as #main
#main "trapclose [quit]"

#main.picasso "down"
#main.picasso "home"

'draw the head
#main.picasso "backcolor cyan ; ellipsefilled 120 200"

'draw the nose
#main.picasso "size 8"
#main.picasso "place 120 100"
```

144

```
#main.picasso "goto 90 130 ; goto 120 140"

'draw the eye
#main.picasso "place 160 100"
#main.picasso "color red"
#main.picasso "circle 15"

'draw the mouth
#main.picasso "color green"
#main.picasso "place 110 200"
#main.picasso "goto 120 190 ; goto 160 220"

'make it all stick
#main.picasso "flush"
wait

[quit]
  close #main
  end
```

Instead of a graphics window we have a plain window and we add a graphicbox to it. The window itself has a handle #main. So, we give the handle #main.picasso to the graphicbox.

In addition to the graphicbox a window can have other controls like buttons, listboxes, etc. or even more graphicbox controls.

We won't cover all the drawing commands here. These are all documented in the Liberty BASIC help file.

Managing drawing segments

The flush command does more than meets the eye. Every time you use flush it takes any new un-flushed drawing operations and seals them all up in a *graphics segment*. A graphics segment is just a collection of drawing operations, and it has a number, which we call a segment ID. Each next graphics segment ID is numbered one higher than the previous one.

How is this segmented graphics model useful? We can get the segment ID number for the segment we are drawing into, and later we can refer to that ID. This is useful mostly so that we can draw a bunch of things over time, keeping some and throwing away others selectively.

Let's see how this sort of code looks by adding segment IDs to our Picasso program:

```
open "Paint a Picasso" for graphics as #picasso
#picasso "trapclose [quit]"

#picasso "down"
#picasso "home"

'draw the head
#picasso "backcolor cyan ; ellipsefilled 120 200"
#picasso "segment head"
#picasso "flush"

'draw the nose
#picasso "size 8"
#picasso "place 120 100"
#picasso "goto 90 130 ; goto 120 140"
#picasso "segment nose"
#picasso "flush"

'draw the eye
#picasso "place 160 100"
#picasso "color red"
#picasso "circle 15"
#picasso "segment eye"
#picasso "flush"

'draw the mouth
#picasso "color green"
#picasso "place 110 200"
#picasso "goto 120 190 ; goto 160 220"
#picasso "segment mouth"
#picasso "flush"

'now delete the nose
#picasso "delsegment "; nose
wait

[quit]
close #picasso
end
```

This looks just like the first Picasso program, that is until you force the window to be redrawn. The portrait will then be missing its nose!

Look at this section of the program:

```
'draw the nose
#picasso "size 8"
#picasso "place 120 100"
#picasso "goto 90 130 ; goto 120 140"
#picasso "segment nose"
#picasso "flush"
```

We added a segment command, which gets the ID number for the graphics segment we are currently drawing in (the segment containing the nose drawing) and puts that ID number into the variable named nose. Then we flush it and a new drawing segment is created.

Later, we use a delsegment command to delete the drawing segment containing the nose using this line:

```
'now delete the nose
#picasso "delsegment "; nose
```

This works because we put the segment ID for the nose drawing in the variable named nose. Just change the variable in this delsegment command to one of the other variables we used to delete some other thing in the portrait, for example:

```
#picasso "delsegment "; head
```

Voila! The invisible man! ;-)

A graph plotting example

Enough with all this Picasso nonsense (it was fun while it lasted)! Let's look at how drawing segments can be useful in a real program. Let's make a little program that draws a sine wave or exponential plot on our command. We will draw a grid in a segment once, and then we'll draw a sine wave or exponential plot in another segment. As we switch between the different kinds of plots, we will delete the segment of the old plot, but keep the drawing segment of the grid so we can redraw it with a single command.

First we'll build a window:

```
'set up a graphing window
graphicbox #main.draw, 4, 4, 300, 300
```

147

```
menu #main, "&Draw", _
  "Sine wave", [sine], _
  "Exponential plot", [exponential]
open "Graph Plotter" for window as #main
#main "trapclose [quit]"
'put the pen down before we do anything else
#main.draw "down"
call drawGrid
wait

[quit]
  close #main
  end
```

We include a call to the drawGrid SUB, which we haven't written yet. *Notice that we break up the MENU command using the underscore.*

Here is our drawGrid SUB:

```
sub drawGrid
  #main.draw "color darkgray"
  for pos = 10 to 300 step 10
    #main.draw "line 0 "; pos; " 300 "; pos
    #main.draw "line "; pos; " 0 "; pos; " 300"
  next pos
  #main.draw "segment gridID"
  print "The grid segment is "; gridID
  #main.draw "flush"
end sub
```

First we set the color of the pen. Our grid will be dark gray.

```
#main.draw "color darkgray"
```

Now in our FOR/NEXT loop, we draw a series of lines spaced 10 apart. We use one loop to draw both vertical and horizontal lines.

```
for pos = 10 to 300 step 10
  #main.draw "line 0 "; pos; " 300 "; pos
  #main.draw "line "; pos; " 0 "; pos; " 300"
next pos
```

Notice how the we have some hard coded values in the line commands. In the places where we need to use the value of the pos variable, we have to make sure to use the variable, and not its name. Think of how the expression would display in the main window if you printed it. Take the

148

following for example:

```
pos = 123
print "line 0 "; pos; " 300 "; pos
```

This prints out as shown below. Do it this way when sending commands to graphics windows and other controls.

```
line 0 123 300 123
```

A common mistake is to put the variable name in the string literal, like so:

```
#main.draw "line 0 pos 300 pos"
```

So, if we used this form with a PRINT command it looks like this:

```
pos = 123
print "line 0 pos 300 pos"
```

And it prints out like this:

```
line 0 pos 300 pos
```

The graphics window expects four numeric values (not variable names), so this isn't going to produce the desired result.

Now, we get to the drawing segment related part.

```
#main.draw "segment gridID"
print "The grid segment is "; gridID
```

The segment command gets the segment ID for the current segment (the one we're drawing into) and puts it into the variable named gridID. Notice that this works differently than the line command which doesn't want variable names. Just so you can see what the segment ID is for our grid, we print it out to the main window.

Finally we flush the drawing operations. This saves all the drawing operations we've just performed into a segment. Then it makes a new segment with its own segment ID (the next in sequence).

```
#main.draw "flush"
```

Now look at the following routine for drawing a sine wave. Type it into the Liberty BASIC editor along with the rest of the code and try it by selecting *Sine wave* from the *Draw* menu. Try it more than once and you'll notice that each time it draws the sine wave it also draws the grid without calling the drawGrid sub.

```
[sine]
  if plotID <> 0 then
    #main.draw "delsegment "; plotID
    #main.draw "redraw"
  end if
  #main.draw "color red ; size 3"
  for x = 1 to 300
    y = 150+75*(sin(x/30))
    #main.draw "set "; x; " "; y
  next x
  #main.draw "segment plotID"
  #main.draw "flush"
  wait
```

The purpose of the first part of the routine might not be immediately clear:

```
  if plotID <> 0 then
    #main.draw "delsegment "; plotID
    #main.draw "redraw"
  end if
```

When the program starts, the value of the variable plotID is 0, so the first time this routine executes it will skip this IF THEN/END IF block. On the other hand, when this routine has been executed at least once, plotID will be non-zero. In that case plotID will hold the segment ID of the last plotted graph. The delsegment command deletes that last drawing segment. This has the added benefit that is also releases memory that holds the drawing information.

Then the redraw command redraws the segments which have not been deleted. In our case, this will only be the segment containing the grid that was drawn when the program started.

Now that we have a nice clean grid, let's plot a new graph:

```
#main.draw "color red ; size 3"
for x = 1 to 300
  y = 150+75*(sin(x/30))
  #main.draw "set "; x; " "; y
next x
```

First we set the pen color to red and the pen size to 3 so that we have a nice bold plot. Then we use a FOR NEXT loop to draw a sine wave. The set command uses the pen to draw a point in the graphicbox at the specified x, y position.

Finally, when we are all done drawing, we get the segment ID of our current drawing and put it into the plot ID variable. Then we flush to seal up the drawing segment.

```
#main.draw "segment plotID"
#main.draw "flush"
wait
```

Now we can add a routine for plotting an exponential graph. It will borrow a lot of code from our sine wave routine:

```
[exponential]
  if plotID <> 0 then
    #main.draw "delsegment "; plotID
    #main.draw "redraw"
  end if
#main.draw "color blue ; size 3"
for x = 1 to 300
  y = (x/300)*x
  #main.draw "set "; x; " "; y
next x
#main.draw "segment plotID"
#main.draw "flush"
wait
```

Add this routine to the existing code in the Liberty BASIC editor and run the program. Try the sine and exponential plots several times each. Cover the window with another on to hide the drawing, then uncover the window. It draws only the grid and the last plot. It doesn't redraw the segments that were deleted.

151

The Simplest Way to Draw With Segments

Drawing with segments the way we demonstrated in the last section is useful, but you must be willing to write the code to make it work. We can simply do away with the extra work and complexity if we use the *cls* command. The cls command deletes all drawing segments and clears the graphics window or graphicbox. Then we can be free to draw everything all at once without thinking about getting segment IDs or deleting them. Here is our graph plotter rewritten to work this way:

```
'set up a graphing window
graphicbox #main.draw, 4, 4, 300, 300
menu #main, "&Draw", _
   "Sine wave", [sine], _
   "Exponential plot", [exponential]
open "Graph Plotter" for window as #main
#main "trapclose [quit]"
'put the pen down before we do anything else
#main.draw "down"
wait

[quit]
  close #main
  end

sub drawGrid
  #main.draw "color darkgray ; size 1"
  for pos = 10 to 300 step 10
    #main.draw "line 0 "; pos; " 300 "; pos
    #main.draw "line "; pos; " 0 "; pos; " 300"
  next pos
end sub

[sine]
  #main.draw "cls"
  call drawGrid
  #main.draw "color red ; size 3"
  for x = 1 to 300
    y = 150+75*(sin(x/30))
    #main.draw "set "; x; " "; y
  next x
  #main.draw "flush"
  wait

[exponential]
  #main.draw "cls"
  call drawGrid
```

152

```
#main.draw "color blue ; size 3"
for x = 1 to 300
  y = (x/300)*x
  #main.draw "set "; x; " "; y
next x
#main.draw "flush"
wait
```

Notice that we still use flush when we're done plotting something. This is
so that we get the automatic redrawing. Also, we needed to added a size 1
command to the drawGrid sub because we use it every time we plot, and
we make the pen thicker when plotting a graph. Try removing the size 1
from the drawGrid sub and see how it affects the appearance of the grid if
you draw more than one time. ;-)

Working with Bitmaps

Sometimes it is helpful to be able to work with an image. Having
something prepared and stored on disk, or even generated by a program
can be a useful thing. For example, look at the *mayhem.bas* program that
comes with Liberty BASIC. It uses four images that come stored in disk
files. These were created using Paintbrush, which is a free drawing
program that comes with WINDOWS. When we load one of these files
into memory using the Liberty BASIC command LOADBMP, it becomes a
bitmap in memory and we can use it in our programs.

What's a bitmap? It's a list of numbers used to paint pixels in a rectangular
area. Each pixel has its own color. Each color is represented by a number.
Put enough pixels together, and you can make a recognizable image. Just
look at your computer screen. There are bitmaps everywhere.

Let's look at a simple program that draws bitmaps on the screen. We'll use
one of the bitmaps from mayhem.bas.

```
'draw a column of tanks
nomainwin
loadbmp "tank", "bmp\ltank.bmp"
open "Tanks" for graphics as #tanks
#tanks "trapclose [quit]"
#tanks "down"
'paint the sky and ground
#tanks "backcolor cyan"
#tanks "place -1 -1 ; boxfilled 400 171"
```

153

```
#tanks "backcolor green"
#tanks "place -1 170 ; boxfilled 400 330"
'draw tanks
for x = 10 to 300 step 40
  #tanks "drawbmp tank "; x; " 150"
next x
#tanks "flush"
wait

[quit]
  close #tanks
  end
```

There are a couple of really important commands in this simple example. The first is LOADBMP:

```
loadbmp "tank", "bmp\ltank.bmp"
```

This loads a bitmap file. The file *ltank.bmp* is located in a folder named *bmp* directly underneath the Liberty BASIC directory. We give it the name "tank" so we can refer to it later. Think of the name as a sort of handle.

Later on we have a FOR/NEXT loop which we use to draw the tanks. The drawbmp command draws a tank at the x,y position we specify.

When we're all done we flush the drawing segment. Bitmap drawing happens in drawing segments just like other graphics operations.

LOADBMP only works with bitmap files with a *bmp* extension, so *jpg*, *gif* and *png* files will not load. If you need to work with these, you will need to convert them to *bmp* format. Newer versions of Windows come with a version of Paintbrush that can load and save in different formats. It may necessary to obtain some add-on application to perform the conversion. Liberty BASIC will unload bitmaps from memory when the program that uses them ends, but you can also unload in your own code, and some people prefer to do it this way. Use the UNLOADBMP command to clean up a bitmap from memory, using the name given to the bitmap when it was loaded. Here is a modification to the [quit] routine of our tanks program that shows how to unload the ltank.bmp file when we exit our program:

```
[quit]
  unloadbmp "tank"
  close #tanks
  end
```

We can load bitmap files, and we can make our own. All we need is to draw an image, and then capture from the graphics window or graphicbox into a bitmap in memory using the getbmp command. Let's modify the tanks program to make a bitmap out of our drawing and display it in a new window:

```
'draw a column of tanks
nomainwin
loadbmp "tank", "bmp\ltank.bmp"
open "Tanks" for graphics as #tanks
#tanks "trapclose [quit]"
#tanks "down"
'paint the sky and ground
#tanks "backcolor cyan"
#tanks "place -1 -1 ; boxfilled 400 171"
#tanks "backcolor green"
#tanks "place -1 170 ; boxfilled 400 330"
'draw tanks
for x = 10 to 300 step 40
  #tanks "drawbmp tank "; x; " 150"
next x
#tanks "flush"
#tanks "getbmp tanks 1 100 100 100"

'open a second window and display our bitmap
open "My own bitmap" for graphics as #myBitmap
#myBitmap "trapclose [quit]"
#myBitmap "down"
#myBitmap "drawbmp tanks 100 100"
#myBitmap "flush"
wait

[quit]
  unloadbmp "tank"
  close #tanks
  close #myBitmap
  end
```

The first thing to notice is the getbmp command. It makes a bitmap and names it "tanks". The bitmap is copied from the graphics window at x,y location 1,100 and it's 100 by 100 pixels large.

Now we open a new graphics window and give it a trapclose handler (the same [quit] routine we use for the first window). We put the pen down, draw the new bitmap and flush the drawing.

155

If we wanted to save our bitmap to a disk file, this is a simple matter of using the BMPSAVE command, which would look like this:

```
bmpsave "tanks", "bmp\tanks.bmp"
```

Capturing Keyboard Activity

Graphics windows and graphics box controls can detect when a user presses any key on the computer's keyboard. This is accomplished by using the *when* command to set up a handler similar to the trapclose command. Look at this very simple example:

```
'demonstrate keypress capturing
open "type something" for graphics as #keyDemo
#keyDemo "trapclose [quit]"
#keyDemo "down"
#keyDemo "when characterInput [keyPressed]"
#keyDemo "setfocus"
wait

[keyPressed]
  'display the key pressed
  #keyDemo "|"; Inkey$
  #keyDemo "flush"
  wait

[quit]
  close #keyDemo
  end
```

Notice this line of code:

```
#keyDemo "when characterInput [keyPressed]"
```

This use of the *when* command tells Liberty BASIC to branch to [keyPressed] whenever a key press is detected. It will only detect a keypress if the graphics area of the window has what is called *input focus*. A simple way to explain this is to consider a window with some textbox controls. The control that has a blinking cursor has the input focus so that key presses are captured by that control. Just like a textbox, a graphics control needs to have input focus if it will detect key presses. We manually give the control input focus, with the following line:

```
#keyDemo "setfocus"
```

Note: You can also force input focus on the graphics control by clicking on it with your mouse. If you later click on some other control, the graphics control will lose the input focus.

When a key press is detected, the Inkey$ will hold information about that key press. So if the A key is pressed, the Inkey$ variable will hold a string "a". If some special key combinations are pressed, Inkey$ will hold what WINDOWS calls *virtual key constants*. Check with the Liberty BASIC help file for more details on how to use this special feature.

Detecting Mouse Actions

Just as we use the *when* command to detect key presses, we can also detect mouse actions. We can detect movement and when a mouse button is pressed or released. Here is a list of the events:

leftButtonDown	- the left mouse button is now down
leftButtonUp	- the left mouse button has been released
leftButtonMove	- the mouse moved while the left button is down
leftButtonDouble	- the left button has been double-clicked
rightButtonDown	- the right mouse button is now down
rightButtonUp	- the right mouse button has been released
rightButtonMove	- the mouse moved while the right button is down
rightButtonDouble	- the right button has been double-clicked
mouseMove	- the mouse moved when no button was down

Now let's use a couple of these to make the world's smallest drawing program:

```
'demonstrate how to handle mouse events
nomainwin
open "smallest drawing program" for graphics as #draw
#draw "trapclose [quit]"
#draw "down"
#draw "place 0 10"
#draw "\Left click to draw\Right click to clear"
#draw "size 2"
#draw "when leftButtonMove [paint]"
#draw "when rightButtonUp [clear]"
wait
```

```
[paint]
  #draw "set "; MouseX; " "; MouseY
  #draw "flush"
  wait

[clear]
  #draw "cls"
  wait

[quit]
  close #draw
  end
```

There are a few important things to note about this example.

Pay attention to the two *when* commands in the first part of the program.
The first one sets up our [paint] routine to execute when the mouse moves
with the left button down. When this routine is called, the mouse position
is placed by Liberty BASIC into the special global variables MouseX and
MouseY. We use these to paint a spot using the *set* command. The second
when command sets up our [clear] routine to be executed when the right
mouse button.

Also, it wasn't necessary to use the *setfocus* command in this example.
This is because when dealing with mouse actions that require the user to
click on the graphics control, focus is set at the moment of the mouse click
so our code doesn't have to set it. :-)

Finally, notice the capitalization of leftButtonMove and rightButtonUp.
Liberty BASIC requires that the correct letter case is used.
LEFTBUTTONMOVE wouldn't work for example.

Exercise

Write a program called STATUS.BAS that displays a graphic for one of
these four status items:

- initial letter
- phone call
- mail information pack
- sale made

A dialog box should contain a graphicbox control to display the graphic, a listbox control to contain a list of the status item, and a statictext control to instruct the user to select a status item.

Four bitmap files are needed for this exercise. You will find these bitmaps in the bmp folder in the Liberty BASIC installation. Their names are LETTER.BMP, CALL.BMP, BROCHURE.BMP, and SALE.BMP. You may use these files to display the graphic for each status item. Here is a short program that shows how to use a listbox control:

This let's take this idea and add some other controls to the dialog box:

```
'show how to use a listbox
nomainwin
'setup some colors
dim color$(5)
color$(0) = "red"
color$(1) = "green"
color$(2) = "blue"
statictext #main, "Pick a color:", 10, 10, 120, 20
listbox #main.colors, color$(), [colorSelected], 10, 35,
120, 60
open "Listbox example" for dialog as #main
#main "trapclose [quit]"
'tell the listbox where to branch on a single-click
#main.colors "singleclickselect [colorSelected]"
wait

[colorSelected]
  #main.colors "selection? selectedColor$"
  notice "You selected " + selectedColor$
  wait

[quit]
  close #main
  end
```

Quiz - Answers are on the next page

1) Before drawing to a graphics window or graphicbox you must use the _____ command.

2) To send more than one command at a time to a graphics window or graphicbox, separate them with a _____.

3) Each use of the flush command creates a new _____ _____.

4) To get the segment ID number for the current drawing segment, use the _____ command.

5) To delete all drawing segments in one shot, use the _____ command.

6) To set up a graphics window or graphicbox to handle key presses, use the _____ _____ command.

7) Key presses are placed as strings into the special variable _____.

8) In order for a graphic window or graphicbox to handle key presses, it must have _____ focus.

9) When handling mouse actions, the x, y position of the mouse is available from the _____ and _____ variables.

Quiz Answers

1) down

2) semicolon

3) drawing segment

4) segment

5) cls

6) when characterInput

7) Inkey$

8) input

9) MouseX, MouseY

Chapter Twelve

Using Random Access Files

For many kinds of applications it is useful to store many of the same kind of thing to disk. Some of the kinds of things that are commonly stored in a file together include customers, contact list entries, sales records, inventory items, video game high scores, and more. Liberty BASIC provides a mechanism for writing and reading this sort of information called *random access files*.

Random access means that you can read or write to any position in the file. You can read or write in any order. This is in contrast to the simpler method called sequential access which limits you to starting at particular point (usually the beginning) and working your way from there, one read or write operation at a time.

Being able to read or write in any order can be really handy. If you know where to find a particular item, you can just jump right there and read it. With sequential access, even if you know that an item is the tenth one, you still have to read the nine items before it.

Our first random access file

Let's create a small program that keeps email addresses for us. We want to keep these items:

```
first name - 20 characters
last name - 20 characters
email address - 30 characters
comment - 50 characters
```

Notice that we figure out how many characters (letters, digits, punctuation, etc.) we need for each item. This is an important restriction of random access files. When using sequential access we don't have to limit the sizes of each item.

These four items together make up what we call a record (or what database programmers call a row). Let's add up the sizes of these items to figure out our record size, which we will need to know when opening the file:

```
20 + 20 + 30 + 50 = 120 characters
```

We'll use the number 120 like so:

```
open "email.dat" for random as #email len = 120
```

Those familiar with sequential access will notice that we don't include the `len = 120` part when opening a sequential file.

After we open the file we need to tell our BASIC program about the items in our record. To do this we use the FIELD statement. Here is what it looks like:

```
field #email, 20 as first$, 20 as last$, _
   30 as email$, 50 as comment$
```

Once we've opened a file and set the field command, we can read or write. Before we can read, we have to write something, so let's do that. We load up the string variables we specified in our FIELD statement with values:

```
firstName$ = "John"
lastName$ = "Doe"
email$ = "johndoe@amnesia.net"
comment$ = "can't remember"
```

Finally, we can write the record using the PUT command. Let's put it in the first position:

```
recordNumber = 1
put #email, recordNumber
```

That's all there is to it! We can write another record by just changing the values of the four string variables and using put again. Also with PUT, we can replace a record by reusing its record number.

Here is an example of the simplest thing that could possibly work. I'll avoid creating a GUI for the program to keep it short.

```
[mainMenu]
  cls
  print "Email contact keeper"
  print
  print "(C)reate new record"
  print "(Q)uit"
  print
  print "Press a letter to choose."

[getChoice]
  choice$ = input$(1)
  if instr("qQ", choice$) <> 0 then end
  if instr("cC", choice$) <> 0 then [createRecord]
  goto [getChoice]

[createRecord]
  cls
  print "Create new record"
  print
  input "Record number?"; record
  input "First name?"; firstName$
  input "Last name?"; lastName$
  input "Email address?"; email$
  input "Comment?"; comment$
  print
  print "(W)rite record, or (A)bort"

[newRecordGetChoice]
  choice$ = input$(1)
  if instr("aA", choice$) <> 0 then [mainMenu]
  if instr("wW", choice$) <> 0 then
    call writeRecord record, firstName$, lastName$, _
      email$, comment$
    goto [mainMenu]
  end if
  goto [newRecordGetChoice]

sub writeRecord record, first$, last$, email$, comment$
  open "email.dat" for random as #email len = 120
  field #email, 20 as first$, 20 as last$, _
    30 as email$, 50 as comment$
  put #email, record
  close #email
end sub
```

This program doesn't do anything but let you create new records, and it forces you to know what record numbers have already been used. We can fix this problem by checking the file size when we open the file using the

LOF( ) function. Let's create a new sub called writeNew which automatically writes to the next new position:

```
sub writeNew first$, last$, email$, comment$
  open "email.dat" for random as #email len = 120
  field #email, 20 as first$, 20 as last$, _
    30 as email$, 50 as comment$
  recordsInFile = lof(#email) / 120
  put #email, recordsInFile+1
  close #email
end sub
```

If we use this we don't need to ask the user for a record number. The writeNew sub calculates the next available record size from the file size. Here is what the program looks like.

```
[mainMenu]
  cls
  print "Email contact keeper"
  print
  print "(C)reate new record"
  print "(Q)uit"
  print
  print "Press a letter to choose."

[getChoice]
  choice$ = input$(1)
  if instr("qQ", choice$) <> 0 then end
  if instr("cC", choice$) <> 0 then [createRecord]
  goto [getChoice]

[createRecord]
  cls
  print "Create new record"
  print
  input "First name?"; firstName$
  input "Last name?"; lastName$
  input "Email address?"; email$
  input "Comment?"; comment$
  print
  print "(W)rite record, or (A)bort"

[newRecordGetChoice]
  choice$ = input$(1)
  if instr("aA", choice$) <> 0 then [mainMenu]
  if instr("wW", choice$) <> 0 then
    call writeNew firstName$, lastName$, _
      email$, comment$
```

166

```
    goto [mainMenu]
  end if
  goto [newRecordGetChoice]

sub writeNew first$, last$, email$, comment$
  open "email.dat" for random as #email len = 120
  field #email, 20 as first$, 20 as last$, _
    30 as email$, 50 as comment$
  recordsInFile = lof(#email) / 120
  put #email, recordsInFile+1
  close #email
end sub
```

Now let's add a really simple routine for showing us the records in our file. To read a record in a random access file, we use the GET command. When using GET, the contents of each item are padded on the end with spaces so that each item returned is as long as specified in the FIELD statement. So if the first item in a record was written as George, it will be set with 14 extra spaces in the first$ variable when read in with the GET statement.

```
  first$ = "George            "
```

Here is a sub that opens our email.dat file, computes how many records it has, and then reads them and prints them to the screen:

```
sub showRecords
  open "email.dat" for random as #email len = 120
  field #email, 20 as first$, 20 as last$, _
    30 as email$, 50 as comment$
  recordsInFile = lof(#email) / 120
  for x = 1 to recordsInFile
    get #email, x
    print first; " "; last$; " "; email$; " "; comment$
  next x
  close #email
end sub
```

When printing out each record, spaces are inserted between each item to keep them from running together. For instance, if my name is Rumplestiltskinapoli Brown, it would print as RumplestiltskinapoliBrown if I didn't put the extra space in. ;-)

To eliminate the extra spaces that are retrieved from the fields we can use a special version of the GET statement called GETTRIM. This will trim out the extra spaces.

And here is the complete program, including the use of GETTRIM:

```
[mainMenu]
  cls
  print "Email contact keeper"
  print
  print "(C)reate new record"
  print "(S)how records"
  print "(Q)uit"
  print
  print "Press a letter to choose."

[getChoice]
  choice$ = input$(1)
  if instr("qQ", choice$) <> 0 then end
  if instr("sS", choice$) <> 0 then
    cls
    call showRecords
    print "Press a key to continue."
    key$ = input$(1)
    goto [mainMenu]
  end if
  if instr("cC", choice$) <> 0 then [createRecord]
  goto [getChoice]

[createRecord]
  cls
  print "Create new record"
  print
  input "First name?"; firstName$
  input "Last name?"; lastName$
  input "Email address?"; email$
  input "Comment?"; comment$
  print
  print "(W)rite record, or (A)bort"

[newRecordGetChoice]
  choice$ = input$(1)
  if instr("aA", choice$) <> 0 then [mainMenu]
  if instr("wW", choice$) <> 0 then
    call writeNew firstName$, lastName$, _
      email$, comment$
    goto [mainMenu]
  end if
  goto [newRecordGetChoice]

sub writeNew first$, last$, email$, comment$
  open "email.dat" for random as #email len = 120
```

```
   field #email, 20 as first$, 20 as last$, _
     30 as email$, 50 as comment$
   recordsInFile = lof(#email) / 120
   put #email, recordsInFile+1
   close #email
end sub

sub showRecords
   open "email.dat" for random as #email len = 120
   field #email, 20 as first$, 20 as last$, _
     30 as email$, 50 as comment$
   recordsInFile = lof(#email) / 120
   for x = 1 to recordsInFile
     gettrim #email, x
     print first$; " "; last$; " "; email$; " "; comment$
   next x
   close #email
end sub
```

Searching for Bobby

Now let's add a facility for finding a record. We want to be able to search the whole record for any text, and we don't want to worry which item the text is in. We also don't want our search to fail if we do a search for "bobby" but the record name is properly capitalized as "Bobby". This routine will look sort of like our showRecords sub, but will have some added stuff:

```
sub findRecords searchFor$
   searchFor$ = upper$(searchFor$)
   open "email.dat" for random as #email len = 120
   recordsInFile = lof(#email) / 120
   for x = 1 to recordsInFile
     field #email, 120 as wholeRecord$
     gettrim #email, x
     if instr(upper$(wholeRecord$), searchFor$) then
       matches = matches + 1
       field #email, 20 as first$, 20 as last$, _
         30 as email$, 50 as comment$
       get #email, x
       print first$; " "; last$; " "; email$; " "; comment$
     end if
   next x
   close #email
   print matches; " matches."
end sub
```

169

See how we can use the FIELD statement to redefine the record we will read on the fly? We loop over each record, defining it first to be a single item of 120 characters called wholeRecord$. Then we use get to read that record, and using the INSTR() function we search it for the string we're interested in. If we get a match, we redefine our record by using FIELD again.

Also notice that by converting our search string into all uppercase with the UPPER$( ) function and by also doing this to wholeRecord$, we are able to find a match even when the case of our search string doesn't match the case of the record. For example, if I'm looking for an email address containing the word "electrode", but the email address stored in the file is "joe@goldElectrode.com", I won't find a match using only INSTR( ), but I will if I also use UPPER$( ):

```
'this won't match it
searchFor$ = "joe@goldElectrode.com"
if instr(searchFor$, "electrode") then
    print "match"
  else
    print "no match"
end if

'this will match it
searchFor$ = "joe@goldElectrode.com"
if instr(upper$(searchFor$), upper$("electrode")) then
    print "match"
  else
    print "no match"
end if
```

In case there is any doubt the UPPER$( ) function converts "joe@goldElectrode.com" to "JOE@GOLDELECTRODE.COM" and "electrode" to "ELECTRODE".

Here is the Email Contact Keeper with the record finder:

```
[mainMenu]
  cls
  print "Email contact keeper"
  print
  print "(C)reate new record"
  print "(S)how records"
  print "(F)ind records"
  print "(Q)uit"
```

```basic
    print
    print "Press a letter to choose."

[getChoice]
  choice$ = input$(1)
  if instr("qQ", choice$) <> 0 then end
  if instr("sS", choice$) <> 0 then
    cls
    call showRecords
    print "Press a key to continue."
    key$ = input$(1)
    goto [mainMenu]
  end if
  if instr("fF", choice$) <> 0 then
    input "Search for?"; searchFor$
    if searchFor$ = "" then [mainMenu]
    cls
    call findRecords searchFor$
    print "Press a key to continue."
    key$ = input$(1)
    goto [mainMenu]
  end if
  if instr("cC", choice$) <> 0 then [createRecord]
  goto [getChoice]

[createRecord]
  cls
  print "Create new record"
  print
  input "First name?"; firstName$
  input "Last name?"; lastName$
  input "Email address?"; email$
  input "Comment?"; comment$
  print
  print "(W)rite record, or (A)bort"

[newRecordGetChoice]
  choice$ = input$(1)
  if instr("aA", choice$) <> 0 then [mainMenu]
  if instr("wW", choice$) <> 0 then
    call writeNew firstName$, lastName$, _
      email$, comment$
    goto [mainMenu]
  end if
  goto [newRecordGetChoice]

sub writeNew first$, last$, email$, comment$
  open "email.dat" for random as #email len = 120
  field #email, 20 as first$, 20 as last$, _
```

171

```
     30 as email$, 50 as comment$
   recordsInFile = lof(#email) / 120
   put #email, recordsInFile+1
   close #email
end sub

sub showRecords
   open "email.dat" for random as #email len = 120
   field #email, 20 as first$, 20 as last$, _
     30 as email$, 50 as comment$
   recordsInFile = lof(#email) / 120
   for x = 1 to recordsInFile
     gettrim #email, x
     print first$; " "; last$; " "; email$; " "; comment$
   next x
   close #email
end sub

sub findRecords searchFor$
   searchFor$ = upper$(searchFor$)
   open "email.dat" for random as #email len = 120
   recordsInFile = lof(#email) / 120
   for x = 1 to recordsInFile
     field #email, 120 as wholeRecord$
     gettrim #email, x
     if instr(upper$(wholeRecord$), searchFor$) then
       matches = matches + 1
       field #email, 20 as first$, 20 as last$, _
         30 as email$, 50 as comment$
       get #email, x
       print first$; " "; last$; " "; email$; " "; comment$
     end if
   next x
   close #email
   print matches; " matches."
end sub
```

This sort of searching works well for small databases of a few hundred items, or even a few thousand, but completely different techniques are needed for very large databases. In the next chapter we'll cover binary searching of random access files.

Quiz – Answers are on the next page

1) With random access files a program can read or write in any
_____.

2) Use the _____ and _____ statements to read and write records to a file.

3) When finished reading or writing to a file, always _____ it.

4) In the following statement, the len = 120 part corresponds to the length of the file's _____.

    open "email.dat" for random as #email len = 120

5) To specify the information items in a record, use the _____ statement.

6) A random access file is made up of one or more
_____.

7) A _____ has one or more fields.

8) An alternative to using GET to read a record is the _____ statement which removes extra spaces from string data.

Answers

1) order

2) GET, PUT

3) close

4) records

5) FIELD

6) records

7) record

8) GETTRIM

Chapter 13

Using Random Access Files - Part 2

In the last chapter we covered the basics of random access files. The techniques we covered are adequate for small applications which only have a few hundred records. It doesn't take long to search for what you need in a random access file when it is small, but if you write an application that will manage thousands of customers, or even just hundreds of customers each having dozens of transaction records (which amounts to thousands of records), then you will need to have a system for speeding things up. We will investigate some ways to do this in this chapter.

What is Binary Search?

One technique for speeding up random access file techniques is called binary search. I'm taking some liberties calling it this since this is usually applied to describe searching a fancy in-memory data structure, but the name does capture the spirit of the technique.

Here's a non-programming example of the technique. You want to look up a word in the dictionary. Do you open the book at the first page and read each word until you find the one you want? Of course not! You crack open the book at some place, usually close to the middle. Sometimes you might try to open the book close to where the word will be found.

You look to see if the word you want is on the page you opened to. It will almost never be there. So if the word is alphabetically before the words on the page, you jump a bunch of pages toward the front of the book. You jump towards the back of the book if the word comes alphabetically after the words you see. Then you make more of these jumps until you find the word you want.

This is a simple technique that most people figure out themselves, and this is how binary searching works. You pick a record in the file and see if it's the one you want. If it isn't then you split the space in two (hence the word binary). Look in the records before or after depending on whether the record comes alphabetically before or after what you are searching for. Then you repeat this until you find the right record.

Sorting

It's important that the records in the file be sorted in order for this technique to work, just like words are sorted in a dictionary. The simplest way to do this is to sort them each time a new record is added.

Extending Our Contact Keeper

Here is the code for the contact keeper program from the last chapter.

```
[mainMenu]
  cls
  print "Email contact keeper"
  print
  print "(C)reate new record"
  print "(S)how records"
  print "(F)ind records"
  print "(Q)uit"
  print
  print "Press a letter to choose."

[getChoice]
  choice$ = input$(1)
  if instr("qQ", choice$) <> 0 then end
  if instr("sS", choice$) <> 0 then
    cls
    call showRecords
    print "Press a key to continue."
    key$ = input$(1)
    goto [mainMenu]
  end if
  if instr("fF", choice$) <> 0 then
    input "Search for?"; searchFor$
    if searchFor$ = "" then [mainMenu]
    cls
    call findRecords searchFor$
    print "Press a key to continue."
    key$ = input$(1)
    goto [mainMenu]
  end if
  if instr("cC", choice$) <> 0 then [createRecord]
  goto [getChoice]
[createRecord]
  cls
  print "Create new record"
  print
  input "First name?"; firstName$
```

```
        input "Last name?"; lastName$
        input "Email address?"; email$
        input "Comment?"; comment$
        print
        print "(W)rite record, or (A)bort"

[newRecordGetChoice]
    choice$ = input$(1)
    if instr("aA", choice$) <> 0 then [mainMenu]
    if instr("wW", choice$) <> 0 then
        call writeNew firstName$, lastName$, _
            email$, comment$
        goto [mainMenu]
    end if
    goto [newRecordGetChoice]

sub writeNew first$, last$, email$, comment$
    open "email.dat" for random as #email len = 120
    field #email, 20 as first$, 20 as last$, _
        30 as email$, 50 as comment$
    recordsInFile = lof(#email) / 120
    put #email, recordsInFile+1
    close #email
end sub

sub showRecords
    open "email.dat" for random as #email len = 120
    field #email, 20 as first$, 20 as last$, _
        30 as email$, 50 as comment$
    recordsInFile = lof(#email) / 120
    for x = 1 to recordsInFile
        gettrim #email, x
        print first$; " "; last$; " "; email$; " "; comment$
    next x
    close #email
end sub

sub findRecords searchFor$
    searchFor$ = upper$(searchFor$)
    open "email.dat" for random as #email len = 120
    recordsInFile = lof(#email) / 120
    for x = 1 to recordsInFile
        field #email, 120 as wholeRecord$
        gettrim #email, x
        if instr(upper$(wholeRecord$), searchFor$) then
            matches = matches + 1
            field #email, 20 as first$, 20 as last$, _
                30 as email$, 50 as comment$
            get #email, x
```

177

```
      print first$; " "; last$; " "; email$; " "; comment$
    end if
  next x
  close #email
  print matches; " matches."
end sub
```

We will add our sorting feature and then we'll also add the binary search method. The first thing is to rewrite the writeNew SUB so that it inserts the new record into the file at the right position to keep the records sorted.

We need to choose which field we will sort by. Let's sort by last name. A lot of the code can remain the same. Examine this code carefully.

```
sub writeNew newFirst$, newLast$, newEmail$, newComment$
  open "email.dat" for random as #email len = 120
  field #email, 20 as first$, 20 as last$, _
    30 as email$, 50 as comment$
  recordsInFile = lof(#email) / 120
  '<<-----------Our new code will go here
  close #email
end sub
```

See that we changed the names of the parameters we pass in? The reason for this will soon become clear. So what code will we put there? We still need to open the file, define the fields, figure out how many records there are and close the file, but we will do a bit more before we can PUT the record.

There are many special kinds of sort routines. The kind we are using in our contact keeper program is called an *insertion sort*.

An insertion sort is best used when there is already a sorted list of things and you just want to add one more thing each time.

First the program must search for the right place for the new item, and then that item is inserted, hence the name.

In order to insert the new item, room must be made for it. This usually involves copying the items over one position, leaving a spot for the new item to be placed. This is like people moving over one seat in order for someone to sit in the middle of a row.

First we need to figure out where the new record goes. The simplest was to do this is by looping through the file from the beginning and reading each record. Once we find the record that has a last name that comes alphabetically after the last name of our new record we have found the spot:

```
for x = 1 to recordsInFile
  get #email, x
  if newLast$ < last$ then  'found the slot!
    'move each record from the x position one
    'position over to make room.
    for copyIndex = recordsInFile to x step -1
      get #email, copyIndex
      put #email, copyIndex + 1
    next copyIndex

    first$ = newFirst$
    last$ = newLast$
    email$ = newEmail$
    comment$ = newComment$
    put #email, x
    success = 1
    exit for   'do not look at more records
  end if
next x
```

First notice the FOR/NEXT loop:

179

```
for x = 1 to recordsInFile
   . . .
next x
```

This loop counts from one to the last record so that we can look for the correct place to insert the record. If the value of recordsInFile is zero then Liberty BASIC will just skip right over the loop. Most versions of BASIC work this way. Then we get the record at that position:

```
get #email, x
```

This will load the fields of record number x into the first$, last$, email$ and comment$ variables. This is why we use different variable names for the parameters that we pass into the SUB (we specify newFirst$, newLast$, newEmail$ and newComment$).

Then we use IF/THEN to see if we've found the right spot to insert the record. If the value of newLast$ is less than the value of last$ (from the current record x) then we want to insert at that position.

```
if newLast$ < last$ then   'found the slot!
```

So now we loop backwards from the last record to the position we want to insert and we copy each record into the record after it. We use GET to read each record and then we use PUT to write each record one position over:

```
'move each record from the x position one
'position over to make room.
for copyIndex = recordsInFile to x step -1
  get #email, copyIndex
  put #email, copyIndex + 1
next copyIndex
```

Notice that the FOR statement ends with step -1. This causes the loop to count backward. Why do we want to do that? Can you guess what would happen if we counted forward?

That's right. The first record copied would overwrite the next one. Then the next loop around would copy the copied information to the next position and so on until all the records held the same information, wiping out all the data to the end of the file. Whoops.

Now we've made room for the new record to be inserted. We don't need to erase what is already there. Simply using PUT to write the new record where it should be will wipe out what was there.

```
first$ = newFirst$
last$ = newLast$
email$ = newEmail$
comment$ = newComment$
put #email, x
```

See how we set the string variables specified in the FIELD statement (first, last$, email$ and comment$) to be the values we passed into the SUB as parameters (newFirst$, newLast$, newEmail$ and newComment$)?

Now that we're finished inserting our new record we do a couple more interesting things. We set the value of a variable named success to 1. We do this so that we will know that we found a place to insert the record. Then we use an EXIT FOR statement to exit the FOR/NEXT loop so that we won't keep on searching for a place to insert (because we already inserted successfully):

```
    success = 1
    exit for   'do not look at more records
  end if
next x
```

Finally after the loop we check the value of the success variable. If it is 0 then we didn't insert the record. That means that it must come alphabetically after all the records in the file. So we add the record onto the end of the file like so:

```
if success = 0 then 'no place found, so add to end
  first$ = newFirst$
  last$ = newLast$
  email$ = newEmail$
  comment$ = newComment$
  put #email, recordsInFile + 1
end if
```

Here's the complete SUB with appropriate blank lines added to help us see the structure of the code:

```
sub writeNew newFirst$, newLast$, newEmail$, newComment$

  open "email.dat" for random as #email len = 120
  field #email, 20 as first$, 20 as last$, _
    30 as email$, 50 as comment$
  recordsInFile = lof(#email) / 120
```

```
for x = 1 to recordsInFile
  get #email, x
  if newLast$ < last$ then  'found the slot!

    'move each record from the x position one
    'position over to make room.
    for copyIndex = recordsInFile to x step -1
      get #email, copyIndex
      put #email, copyIndex + 1
    next copyIndex

    first$ = newFirst$
    last$ = newLast$
    email$ = newEmail$
    comment$ = newComment$
    put #email, x
    success = 1
    exit for  'do not look at more records

  end if
next x

if success = 0 then 'no place found, so add to end
  first$ = newFirst$
  last$ = newLast$
  email$ = newEmail$
  comment$ = newComment$
  put #email, recordsInFile + 1
end if

close #email

end sub
```

This replaces the SUB of the same name in our contact keeper program.

To test this, run the program and try adding some new records. Enter them out of order by last name. Then use the show records option in the program's menu. The records should appear sorted by last name.

Adding a Binary Search Routine

The next step is to add a routine for looking up an entry by last name. The program already has a find feature which searches on a partial match, and it does it's work by searching from the beginning of the file to the end. This new routine will search for an exact match and it will do so using the binary search technique we compared to looking up a word in a dictionary.

Let's start the code for our SUB like so:

```
sub lastNameQuickSearch searchFor$
  searchFor$ = upper$(searchFor$)
  open "email.dat" for random as #email len = 120
  field #email, 20 as first$, 20 as last$, _
    30 as email$, 50 as comment$
  recordsInFile = lof(#email) / 120
```

Nothing surprising here. This is very similar to other code we've already written. The only remarkable bit is the use of the UPPER$( ) function. We convert the last name we will search for to uppercase. When each record is written we will also use the UPPER$( ) function on the last name in that record so that we can compare successfully, for example if the record on disk is capitalized but the user of the program types the name in lowercase. This is known as *case insensitive search*. It's easy to overlook this feature which is used by popular online search engines like Google.

Now have a look at the next bit of code. We will not search if there are no records in the file.

```
if recordsInFile = 0 then
  print "There are no records to search."
else
  'search code goes in here
end if
```

The code for searching will go between the ELSE and the END IF.

```
if recordsInFile = 1 then
  record = 1
else
  upperLimit = recordsInFile + 1
  lowerLimit = 1
end if
```

If there is only one record in the file we just set record to 1 in order to point right at it. Otherwise we set an upper limit and a lower limit which at the beginning will be the entire range of records. As we search through the records these limits will be adjusted.

If we have 50 records, our initial limits will be 1 and 51. If we examine record 25 and discover that what we're searching for is alphabetically before what's in that record, our new upperLimit becomes 25. So now

183

we've split the search space in half (binary search, remember?) and now we'll recompute the record number based on the new limits. The upper limit is now 25. Divide the sum of the lower and upper limits to find the next record to look at. The integer part of 25 + 1 / 2 is 13. Now we look at record 13 and we see that what we're searching for is alphabetically after what's in that record. So our new lower limit is 13. And so on until we find the record we want or we discover that it doesn't exist.

Why is the initial upper limit 51 and not 50? Because the technique we use determines the next record to look at by adding the lower and upper limits and dividing by two. This means that we will never search the last record unless we define the upper limit to be one more than the number of records.

Here is the search loop:

```
while searchComplete = 0 and searchFailed = 0
  record = int((upperLimit + lowerLimit) / 2)
  gettrim #email, record
  upperLast$ = upper$(last$)
  if searchFor$ = upperLast$ then
    searchComplete = 1
  else
    if searchFor$ < upperLast$ then
      upperLimit = record
    else
      lowerLimit = record
    end if
    if lastRecord = record then
      searchFailed = 1
    end if
    lastRecord = record
  end if
wend
```

Notice how our WHILE/WEND loop is controlled by two variables named searchComplete and searchFailed. If we find a matching record we set searchComplete to 1. If we keep shrinking our search space until the record is the same for two iterations of the loop in a row (see the use of lastRecord), this means the search has failed to find a match.

After the loop is finished we test to see if the search has failed. We either display a failure message, or else we show the record that matches, like so:

```
if searchFailed = 1 then
```

184

```
      print "Last name not found: "; searchFor$
    else
      print first$; " "; last$; " "; email$; " "; comment$
    end if
```

Here is the complete code for the lastNameQuickSearch SUB:

```
sub lastNameQuickSearch searchFor$
  searchFor$ = upper$(searchFor$)
  open "email.dat" for random as #email len = 120
  field #email, 20 as first$, 20 as last$, _
    30 as email$, 50 as comment$
  recordsInFile = lof(#email) / 120
  if recordsInFile = 0 then
    print "There are no records to search."
  else
    if recordsInFile = 1 then
      record = 1
    else
      upperLimit = recordsInFile + 1
      lowerLimit = 1
    end if
    while searchComplete = 0 and searchFailed = 0
      record = int((upperLimit + lowerLimit) / 2)
      gettrim #email, record
      upperLast$ = upper$(last$)
      if searchFor$ = upperLast$ then
        searchComplete = 1
      else
        if searchFor$ < upperLast$ then
          upperLimit = record
        else
          lowerLimit = record
        end if
        if lastRecord = record then
          searchFailed = 1
        end if
        lastRecord = record
      end if
    wend
    if searchFailed = 1 then
      print "Last name not found: "; searchFor$
    else
      print first$; " "; last$; " "; email$; " "; comment$
    end if
  end if
  close #email
end sub
```

What's on the menu?

I'll have one of those quick searches with a little cole slaw on the side. ;-)
okay, we just need to change our menu to handle our new search option.
Here's one way we can do that:

```
print "(C)reate new record"
print "(S)how records"
print "(F)ind records"
print "(L)ast name quick search"
print "(Q)uit"
```

And we also need to add some code to use our lastNameQuickSearch
SUB, so let's add the following code to the end of the [getChoice] routine:

```
if instr("1L", choice$) <> 0 then
  input "Search for last name?"; lastName$
  if lastName$ = "" then [mainMenu]
  cls
  call lastNameQuickSearch lastName$
  print "Press a key to continue."
  key$ = input$(1)
  goto [mainMenu]
end if
goto [getChoice]
```

Here is the complete source code for the program with our quick search
feature added:

```
[mainMenu]
  cls
  print "Email contact keeper"
  print
  print "(C)reate new record"
  print "(S)how records"
  print "(F)ind records"
  print "(L)ast name quick search"
  print "(Q)uit"
  print
  print "Press a letter to choose."

[getChoice]
  choice$ = input$(1)
  if instr("qQ", choice$) <> 0 then end
  if instr("sS", choice$) <> 0 then
    cls
    call showRecords
```

```
      print "Press a key to continue."
      key$ = input$(1)
      goto [mainMenu]
    end if
    if instr("fF", choice$) <> 0 then
      input "Search for?"; searchFor$
      if searchFor$ = "" then [mainMenu]
      cls
      call findRecords searchFor$
      print "Press a key to continue."
      key$ = input$(1)
      goto [mainMenu]
    end if
    if instr("cC", choice$) <> 0 then [createRecord]
    if instr("lL", choice$) <> 0 then
      input "Search for last name?"; lastName$
      if lastName$ = "" then [mainMenu]
      cls
      call lastNameQuickSearch lastName$
      print "Press a key to continue."
      key$ = input$(1)
      goto [mainMenu]
    end if
    goto [getChoice]

[createRecord]
    cls
    print "Create new record"
    print
    input "First name?"; firstName$
    input "Last name?"; lastName$
    input "Email address?"; email$
    input "Comment?"; comment$
    print
    print "(W)rite record, or (A)bort"

[newRecordGetChoice]
    choice$ = input$(1)
    if instr("aA", choice$) <> 0 then [mainMenu]
    if instr("wW", choice$) <> 0 then
      call writeNew firstName$, lastName$, _
        email$, comment$
      goto [mainMenu]
    end if
    goto [newRecordGetChoice]

sub writeNew newFirst$, newLast$, newEmail$, newComment$

    open "email.dat" for random as #email len = 120
```

187

```
    field #email, 20 as first$, 20 as last$, _
      30 as email$, 50 as comment$
    recordsInFile = lof(#email) / 120

    for x = 1 to recordsInFile
      get #email, x
      if newLast$ < last$ then   'found the slot!

        'move each record from the x position one
        'position over to make room.
        for copyIndex = recordsInFile to x step -1
          get #email, copyIndex
          put #email, copyIndex + 1
        next copyIndex

        first$ = newFirst$
        last$ = newLast$
        email$ = newEmail$
        comment$ = newComment$
        put #email, x
        success = 1
        exit for   'do not look at more records

      end if
    next x

    if success = 0 then 'no place found, so add to end
      first$ = newFirst$
      last$ = newLast$
      email$ = newEmail$
      comment$ = newComment$
      put #email, recordsInFile + 1
    end if

    close #email

end sub

sub showRecords
  open "email.dat" for random as #email len = 120
  field #email, 20 as first$, 20 as last$, _
    30 as email$, 50 as comment$
  recordsInFile = lof(#email) / 120
  for x = 1 to recordsInFile
    gettrim #email, x
    print first$; " "; last$; " "; email$; " "; comment$
  next x
  close #email
end sub
```

```
sub findRecords searchFor$
  searchFor$ = upper$(searchFor$)
  open "email.dat" for random as #email len = 120
  recordsInFile = lof(#email) / 120
  for x = 1 to recordsInFile
    field #email, 120 as wholeRecord$
    gettrim #email, x
    if instr(upper$(wholeRecord$), searchFor$) then
      matches = matches + 1
      field #email, 20 as first$, 20 as last$, _
        30 as email$, 50 as comment$
      get #email, x
      print first$; " "; last$; " "; email$; " "; comment$
    end if
  next x
  close #email
  print matches; " matches."
end sub

sub lastNameQuickSearch searchFor$
  searchFor$ = upper$(searchFor$)
  open "email.dat" for random as #email len = 120
  field #email, 20 as first$, 20 as last$, _
    30 as email$, 50 as comment$
  recordsInFile = lof(#email) / 120
  if recordsInFile = 0 then
    print "There are no records to search."
  else
    if recordsInFile = 1 then
      record = 1
    else
      upperLimit = recordsInFile + 1
      lowerLimit = 1
    end if
    while searchComplete = 0 and searchFailed = 0
      record = int((upperLimit + lowerLimit) / 2)
      gettrim #email, record
      upperLast$ = upper$(last$)
      if searchFor$ = upperLast$ then
        searchComplete = 1
      else
        if searchFor$ < upperLast$ then
          upperLimit = record
        else
          lowerLimit = record
        end if
        if lastRecord = record then
          searchFailed = 1
```

189

```
      end if
      lastRecord = record
    end if
  wend
  if searchFailed = 1 then
    print "Last name not found: "; searchFor$
  else
    print first$; " "; last$; " "; email$; " "; comment$
  end if
  end if
  close #email
end sub
```

Variations on a Theme

There are other ways to approach the binary search idea. Let's look at a couple.

Index Files

Instead of sorting the data file every time you add a new record, you can have a second file with records having two values. Each row has the contents of the field (last name for example) you want to search, and that record's index position in the data file. This second file is called an index file. When you add a new record to the data file you just stick it on the end (the data file is not sorted) and then you add a new record to the index file, but this file is kept sorted. You can use the index file to quickly search for information in the data file.

So what is the benefit of this? It seems like you have to maintain two files, and the result is the same as with one file? This approach does have an advantage. You can have more than one index file. With the single data file you can only sort it by one field. With external index files you can have one for each field that you want to do a quick search for.

Delayed Sorting

If a data file grows very large so that it has many thousands of records, it may become objectionable if the time to sort when adding new records becomes more than a few seconds. What can you do about this?

One way to deal with this is to have two files. One large, and one small. New records go into the small file. When you need to get the information you use the binary search method to look in the large file, and just loop over the small file and look at each record to search the small one. Then once the small file reaches a certain size or maybe at the end of the day you add the rows from the small file into the big one and sort it then.

Another way to do this is to add new records onto the end of the data file, but don't sort right away. When the new record causes the size of the file to reach a round number like 100, 200, 300, etc. then you stop and sort the file then. This means you will have a bunch of unsorted records on the end of the file. To search them you use the binary search for record 1 to the rounded number (for example that would be 200 if you 235 records), and scan the remaining 35 records one at a time to search those.

Exercise

Modify the writeNew SUB so that it uses a binary search technique to find the correct slot to insert the new record instead of searching one record at a time from the beginning of the file.

Quiz – Answers on the next page

1) One good way to insert one item into a sorted list is called an
_____ sort.

2) A search technique that splits a file into smaller and smaller regions
until it finds a match is called _____ search.

3) A sorted file used to speed up search in another file is called an
_____ file.

4) The UPPER$( ) function was used in this chapter to demonstrate a
technique for case _____ searching.

5) Without using index files only one field can be used for binary
searching because the data file can only be _____ by one
field at a time.

Answers

1) insertion

2) binary

3) index

4) insensitive

5) sorted

Alphabetical Index